Household Waste Management

Marianna Gilli · Susanna Mancinelli
Francesco Nicolli

Household Waste Management

Some Insights from Behavioural Economics

Marianna Gilli
Department of Economics and
 Management
University of Ferrara
Ferrara, Italy

Susanna Mancinelli
Department of Economics and
 Management
University of Ferrara
Ferrara, Italy

Francesco Nicolli
European University Institute
Florence, Italy

and

Department of Political and
 International Sciences
University of Siena
Siena, Italy

ISBN 978-3-319-97809-3   ISBN 978-3-319-97810-9   (eBook)
https://doi.org/10.1007/978-3-319-97810-9

Library of Congress Control Number: 2018950051

This Palgrave Pivot imprint is published by the registered company Springer Nature Switzerland AG
The registered company address is: Gewerbestrasse 11, 6330 Cham, Switzerland

CONTENTS

LIST OF FIGURES

LIST OF TABLES

CHAPTER 1

Introduction

Abstract This chapter introduces the purpose of the book as well as the
waste management system in the EU, and the concept of circular economy. The aim of the book is to offer insights about the main determinants of individual attitudes toward waste reduction and recycling. The
book collects some of the main contributions of the economic literature
on the topic as well as two original empirical investigations that intend
to verify the role of different determinants on individuals' waste-related
behaviours, and their possible interactions. The book enriches the scarce
literature on the determinants of waste behaviours and of the efficacies of
waste policies and provides some important suggestion for policymaking.

Keywords Waste management · Circular economy · Motivations
Pro-environmental behaviour

In addition to climate change mitigation, waste management and disposal are among the main issues in policymakers' environmental agendas.
The European Union, for example, has issued various directives intended
to promote the use of alternative disposal methodologies. The most
important step in that transition has been the waste framework directive (2008/98/EC), which presents a political and conceptual framework that should guide the evolution of European waste management
towards a 'recycling society'. A milestone of that first approach was the
consolidation of the so-called waste hierarchy, i.e. a ranking of waste

© The Author(s) 2018
M. Gilli et al., *Household Waste Management*,
https://Doi.org/10.1007/978-3-319-97810-9_1

1

management choices, in which landfills are considered to be the worst possible option, and prevention is the preferred option. A second step in this long path is the promulgation of the circular economy package, which poses the basis for a new definition of the European Economic System. In a few words, by circular economy, the European Parliament means a new concept of economy in which production is a circular flow that is based on a solid combination of reuse, repair, refurbishing and recycling, with the final aim of turning waste into resources. A similar approach has also been taken by Japan, which has recently stressed the need to promote a transition towards a Sound Material-Cycle Society,[1] a new concept of an economic system based on waste minimization, recycling and resource reuse, and by the US, which has recently highlighted the key role of waste prevention and recycling as cornerstones of the country's waste management strategy.[2]

The success of these new and ambitious political approaches, which focus on waste reduction, separate collection, reuse and recycling, heavily depends on the contributions of citizens and households. This means, in other terms, that studying and understanding waste-related behaviours is becoming increasingly relevant. Actually, a relevant strand of economic literature has widely investigated how individuals' reduction and recycling decisions respond to waste policies and to the diverse incentive devices. In this context an always increasing attention is drawn on individual motivations at the basis of waste management, with the purpose of considering the role of both monetary and non-monetary incentives towards a pro-environmental behaviour.

Individual behaviour in waste management is the focus of the book. Our aim is to offer insights about the main determinants of individual attitudes towards waste reduction and recycling, relying on some of the main contributions of the economic literature on the topic. Moreover, we offer two original empirical investigations that intend to deeply verify the role of different relevant determinants on individuals' waste-related behaviours, and also their possible interactions.

---

[1] See the documentation in the 'Sound Material-Cycle Society', section of the Japanese Ministry of the Environment web site: http://www.env.go.jp/en/recycle/smcs/index.html.

[2] See for example the 'RCRA's Critical Mission & the Path Forward', which is available at the Environmental Protection Agency (EPA) web page: https://www.epa.gov/rcra/resource-conservation-and-recovery-act-rcra-overview.

To the pursuit of our goal, the book is organized into four chapters. Chapter 2 is devoted to the analysis of individuals' intrinsic and extrinsic motivations behind pro-social behaviours, focusing particularly on the waste management context. Drivers different from the pecuniary ones are considered to incentivize people to undertake waste reduction and recycling. The possible interrelationships between the two waste management behaviours are investigated and some field experiment studies have been reported that contribute to a better understanding of the motivations that lead people to adopt pro-social behaviour in the waste realm. Chapter 3 complements the first one in that it aims at investigating waste policies that may affect individuals' behaviour towards waste minimization and recycling. Both market base mechanisms, as unit-based pricing for unsorted waste, and technical policies, as adoption of curbside or drop-off systems are considered. The strength and weakness of each mechanism as drivers of people's waste-related behaviours are highlighted. Chapter 4 offers an empirical investigation of individual motivations behind waste reduction and recycling. More specifically, it aims at verifying if one type of motivation (intrinsic and extrinsic) is more correlated with one of the two behaviours (minimization and recycling) or the other. Using Eurobarometer data, we note that extrinsic motivation has a higher effect on recycling habits than on minimization behaviour whilst the reverse is true for intrinsic motivation. Moreover, intrinsic motivation plays a role for the recycling of particular kinds of waste such as hazardous waste. Chapter 5, finally, considers both motivations and waste policies as determinants of people's waste-related behaviour, with a specific focus on recycling. It analyses how waste collection policies can incentivize houschold recycling behaviours and whether individual motivations are capable of crowding-in policy efficacies, especially when the efforts required by agents are high. We exploit a new survey of 618 Italian families that reports information on the opinions and stated actual recycling behaviours of the respondents with respect to five different waste materials.

We do believe this work is valuable for several reasons. From an academic perspective, it enriches the still rather scarce literature on the determinants of waste behaviours and of the efficacies of waste policies with two original contributions, one at European level, and another one for a big European Country: Italy. From a policymaker perspective, we believe it provides some important suggestions. Firstly, it shows as individual motivations, both intrinsic and extrinsic, are positively correlated (to a different extent) to minimization and recycling performances. Moreover, individual motivations may overcome possible weaknesses in waste policies, for example, by reducing the negative effects of 'distance' between households and recycling centres. Secondly, it shows that collection policies oriented at reducing time opportunity costs increase household recycling performances, and it is extremely relevant that policies are efficiently managed, lest discouraging effects occur. Finally, it shows the importance of elements like information and specific knowledge, which, increasing citizens' awareness on waste issues, are a necessary precondition of the efficacy of both recycling and minimization policies. We do strongly believe that this information can help policymakers in the process of designing a successful future waste policy framework.

CHAPTER 2

Individual Motivations
and Waste-Related Behaviours

Abstract This chapter is devoted to the analysis of individuals' intrinsic and extrinsic motivations behind pro-social behaviours, focusing particularly on the waste management context. Drivers different from the pecuniary ones are considered to incentivize people to undertake waste reduction and recycling. The possible interrelationships between the two waste management behaviours are investigated and some field experiment studies have been reported that contribute to a better understanding of the motivations that lead people to adopt pro-social behaviour in the waste realm.

Keywords Waste management · Motivations · Pro-social behaviour

2.1 INTRODUCTION

The economic literature has widely recognized and accepted the idea that motives which induce people to engage in pro-social behaviour may go beyond purely economic reward. In this respect, the economic research is making use of psychological studies for a better understanding of the individuals' choices that goes beyond the classic framework of human being only driven by selfish monetary motives. Following this direction, several studies consider individual motivations when the pro-social behaviour is pro-environment. In these studies,

© The Author(s) 2018
M. Gilli et al., *Household Waste Management*,
https://doi.org/10.1007/978-3-319-97810-9_2

the non-pecuniary levers of environmental behaviour are attributed to different behavioural 'norms' such as altruism, social or moral norms, warm-glow and eco-centrism. In the context of waste recycling and reduction, analysis of pecuniary and non-pecuniary incentives is more challenging if we compare waste realms to other environmental issues, since the related pro-environmental actions generally present low individual benefits and high opportunity time costs.

Individual decisions about what to buy and how to dispose of goods play a fundamental role in waste prevention and recycling programmes, and purely economic incentives may result not sufficiently adequate to lever individual actions towards pro-environmental behaviours. Thus, a good understanding of the motivations influencing people's preferences and behaviours is essential to tackling the problem of waste effectively.

The present chapter is devoted to the analysis of the economic literature on pro-social behaviour with a specific focus on the waste management realm.

2.2   PRO-SOCIAL BEHAVIOUR: INTRINSIC AND EXTRINSIC MOTIVATIONS

At least four groups of theories may be identified in the economic literature on pro-social behaviour (Meier 2007). In the first group of theories, people's pro-social behaviour is explained with a view to achieving a private or material reward, such as tax breaks in the case of donations or the creation of social networks in the case of voluntary work (Olson 1965). The second group of theories explains the possibility that people care about the well-being of others on the basis of three reasons: first, people's own utility function is directly and positively influenced by the well-being of others, as in the case of Becker's (1974) pure altruists and their donation to a public good; second, people perceive a 'warm glow' from their pro-social behaviour, as in the case of Andreoni's (1989, 1990) impure altruists who, by contributing to the public good, 'get some private good benefit from their gift per se, like a warm glow' (Andreoni 1989, pp. 1448–1449); third, people dislike inequality and hence behave altruistically towards those worse off than themselves, as in Fehr and Schmidt (1999). The third group of theories considers individuals' sense of reciprocity as lever of their pro-social behaviour, that hence depends on the behaviour of others within a given group (Rabin 1993; Fehr and Gächter 2000). Finally, the fourth group refers to social norms and reputational concerns as triggers for people's pro-social behaviour (Bènabou and Tirole 2006).

Pro-social behaviours are, hence, driven by intrinsic and extrinsic motivations. A generally accepted definition of intrinsic motivations comes from psychology (Deci 1975) and identifies the peculiarity of an intrinsic motive in the absence of an external reward, and as a motivation that comes from 'within the person's attitude'. According to Deci (1971, p. 105), 'one is said to be intrinsically motivated to perform an activity when one receives no apparent reward except the activity itself'. On the other hand, extrinsic motivation comes from outside the person.

On this basis, motives such as pure altruism or 'warm glow' may be included in the set of intrinsic motivations, since their rewards are purely internal, derived from the donor's own knowledge of her pro-social behaviour. Becker's (1974) altruists and Andreoni's (1989, 1990) impure altruists are individuals characterized by intrinsic motivations. It is not relevant if a contributor to a public good, only considers the maximization of social welfare, complying with an ideal of social welfare function, or if instead in pursuing the maximization of social welfare, she also aims at maximizing her own utility function through the 'warm-glow' received from giving. What must be emphasized is that agents driven by intrinsic motivations are interested in neither pecuniary rewards nor peer (social) approval (Cecere et al. 2014). Intrinsically motivated people do not expect any external rewards for their actions but merely obey 'individualistic based altruism' (e.g. actions driven by option values, bequest values, inter-generational preferences, etc.) and the utility they perceive is due to purely internal factors.

Reasons that are ascribable to 'perceived external pressure' may instead be included in the category of extrinsic motivations. Motivations related to the individual's need to gain external rewards, either economic or in term of social appraisal enter this category. Behaviours that are instrumental in obtaining an external material reward, such as tax breaks are surely triggered by extrinsic motivations. Reciprocity, social norms and reputational concerns instead necessitate further examination, since they do not appear to only come from within the person. For what especially concerns social norms a straight and clear distinction is difficult to operate. In fact, people keen to conform to a socially shared perception of an ideal form of pro-social behaviour are moved both by the desire to achieve a good self-image (essentially intrinsic) and to gain the respect and approval of others (essentially extrinsic). People behave pro-socially in order to signal their good traits to both themselves and others. In Bènabou and Tirole (2006) the image component is a function of individuals' concerns for their reputation and may be affected by the visibility of their actions. Obviously, the more hidden the action the less relevant the social approval (Ariely et al. 2009). More generally, a crucial property of external motivation is its dependency on the visibility of the pro-social behaviour. No external rewards will be perceived if the behaviour is hidden.

2.2.1   Crowding-In and Crowding-Out Effects

The distinction between intrinsic and extrinsic motivations and the analysis of their possible interactions provides useful grounds to better understand which are the incentives that drive people towards pro-social behaviour. In fact, since pro-social behaviour is costly, on the one hand its magnitude typically increases with external monetary incentives according to the relative price effect. On the other hand, however, through what can be defined as a 'motivation crowding-out effect', monetary incentives could decrease intrinsic motivations at the basis of the pro-social behaviour. The final net effect will depend on the magnitude of the two effects and, under specific conditions, the relative price effect can even be reversed.

Since the Titmuss's (1970) study about blood donation, in which he showed that paying for blood donations could undermine the dominant social norm about voluntary contribution and reduce the willingness to donate, the motivation's crowding-out effect has been widely exploited in the economic literature.[1] Main conclusions are that under different conditions external interventions may crowd-out or crowd-in intrinsic motivation, or leave it unaffected. Frey and Jegen (2001) identify 'controlling activities' as the psychological condition under which external incentives crowd-out individuals' intrinsic motivations and 'perception of supportive activities' as the psychological condition under which external incentives crowd-in intrinsic motivation. External incentives can be detrimental to pro-social behaviour because these may threaten both the self-determination and the self-esteem of an individual. In other words, the external intervention may either lead a person to perceive that the

---

[1] For an exhaustive survey, see Frey and Jegen (2001) and Bowles and Polania-Reyes (2012).

control on her values has shifted from inside her to outside her (impaired self-determination) or to perceive that her internal motivation is not externally recognized (impaired self-esteem). In this last situation, the incentives may reveal that the proponent doesn't trust the recipient's intrinsic motivations, and could be read as 'bad signal' (Gneezy et al. 2011). Bowles and Polania-Reyes (2012) highlight that on the one hand external, especially monetary, incentives may induce moral disengagement, activating payoff-maximizing modes of thought. But, on the other hand, incentives may crowd-in intrinsic motivations, affecting how people learn new social preferences. In voluntary work, for instance, the introduction of monetary incentives shifts the perception related to the individual's decision. Human beings calculate the costs and benefits of a job, namely if it is worth working for the wage received. In the absence of external monetary incentives, people work for an internal moral reward—the warm-glow. If the external monetary incentive is not sufficiently high, it might be that the crowding-out effect overwhelms the relative price effect, so that volunteers who receive a low monetary reward work less than both people who receive large rewards and people who receive no reward at all (Frey and Goette 1999; Gneezy and Rustichini 2000a). Bolle and Otto (2010) explain the existence and persistence of crowding-out and crowding-in effects on the basis of the signals offered by prices. In their study the introduction of a monetary incentive for people who show pro-social actions is a signal (price) of the value of their action. So, if a monetary incentive is introduced, the crowding-out (crowding-in) effect might prevail if the price offered is considerably lower (higher) than the value estimate people have of their behaviour.

Intrinsic motivations can be crowded-out by pecuniary incentives only when a previously-set non-monetary relationship is transformed into an explicitly monetary one. If behaviours are triggered by external pecuniary rewards from the beginning, the increase in external incentives will be likely to increase effort as predicted by standard theory.

When individuals' motivation for pro-social behaviour is social approval, visibility of the action matters (Ariely et al. 2009). When the action is visible, the presence of economic incentives may induce suspicion in society and a pro-social behaviour initially appraised by peers may be considered as triggered by selfish maximizing motivations, so that social approval can be converted to social stigma (Bènabou and Tirole 2006). In this case the crowding-out effect prevails. Instead, if the action is hidden, the relative price effect (which is independent of visibility) increases pro-social behaviour and a crowding-in effect prevails.

2.3   Motivations and Waste Management

A relevant strand of economic literature has recognized the importance of individual motivations, as alternative to monetary incentives, when the pro-social behaviour is pro-environment.[2] We believe that waste-related issues are particularly intriguing in this framework for the specific characteristics of the two main waste-related behaviours: waste reduction and recycling. For what concerns the latter, the associated individual actions typically require high effort and opportunity cost of time and low individual benefits. In this situation monetary incentives alone may result too low to guarantee increased efforts by people. For what concerns waste reduction, instead, the main associated individual action should consist of reduced consumption of materials that are subsequently thrown away. This is particularly evident when dealing with food waste: what is discarded is usually what has been purchased in excess and not consumed. In this situation, the monetary incentive should already come from saving due to 'not to buy in excess'. Hence, something more than merely pecuniary drivers must be explored to incentivize people to undertake this pro-environmental behaviour.

It is almost intuitive from above that waste reduction and recycling represent different dimensions of the waste management behaviours and may well be driven by the two sets of motivations (extrinsic and intrinsic) in different ways. The first relevant difference between the two waste-oriented behaviours pertains to their degree of visibility: whilst recycling may be visible to '*neighbours*' eyes',[3] waste reduction is a more private action which is unlikely to be observable by others (Barr 2007; Cecere et al. 2014). In fact, it typically involves private decisions as to not buy, or purchasing items that result in less waste, or reuse and repair something (Bortoleto 2014) or hidden actions as home composting. On the basis of the considerations reported in the previous section, it is more conceivable that the more visible recycling behaviour is induced by both extrinsic and intrinsic motivations, whilst the more hidden waste

---

[2] About the importance of behavioral economics for environmental economics, see Kesternich et al. (2017) and the literature review there presented.

[3] Putting the containers at the curbside, for instance, is visible to the others.

reduction behaviour is mainly related to intrinsic motivations (Cecere et al. 2014). Many studies on the subject confirm this insight.[4] Barr (2007), for instance, among the several factors that influence waste management behaviour and that are classified in three groups of independent variables (environmental values, situational variables and psychological factors), finds that whilst waste reduction behaviour is due to personal environmental values, recycling is fundamentally a normative behaviour. Waste minimization is driven by intrinsic value in nature, which instead have negligible effects on recycling, governed mainly by normative and convenience-based factors.[5] According to Ebreo and Vining (2001) the two waste-related behaviours are different dimensions of behaviour with different correlates and internal values. General concerns for the environment are individuated to be the main motives for waste reduction. Recycling behaviour, instead, is mainly motivated by individual concerns for the future. The fundamental role of intrinsic motivations as drivers of waste minimization is shown also in Cecere et al. (2014) for the specific case of food waste. In their study, instead, extrinsic motivations do not play a significant role to incentivize waste reduction behaviour. In Abbott et al. (2013), intrinsic motivations are not so relevant to stimulate recycling behaviour. In their analysis on the link between the quality of recycling facilities and recycling effort, no significant relationship is found between warm-glow and recycling behaviour, which is conversely driven by social norms and peer effect. On the contrary, the possibility that people undertake recycling activities for more intrinsic motivations has been shown by several studies (Brekke et al. 2003, 2010; Hage et al. 2009; Halvorsen 2008). Berglund (2006), for instance, shows that people with higher Green Moral Index (the measure for intrinsic motivations) have a lower willingness to pay to let someone else take over the waste recycling activity. Similarly Kinnaman (2006) suggests that recycling is increased more by warm-glow incentives than by unit-based pricing, to the point that households may even be willing to pay for the opportunity to recycle.[6] The willingness to pay to recycle at home

---

[4]The existing literature includes several studies about motivations and recycling and fewer about motivations and waste reduction.

[5]Among these factors Barr (2007) includes the access to a curbside recycling facilities and the awareness of these facilities.

[6]'Recycling is something parents and children feel good about, and for this reason households may be willing to pay for the mere opportunity to recycle' (Kinnaman 2006, p. 222).

is investigated in Czajkowski et al. (2017) and their main finding is that the willingness to pay is associated with moral or intrinsic norms. Using U.S. data, Viscusi et al. (2011) show that in the recycling of plastic water bottles, 'private' values, such as individual pro-environmental behaviour, prove more effective than external norms and economic incentives. Finally, empirical outcomes in D'Amato et al. (2016) show that warm-glow positively affects waste reduction and has no direct effect on recycling, but only an indirect effect due to the relationship of complementarity detected between the two waste-related behaviours. Recycling is, instead, directly affected by social norms.

In the studies above considered, whilst recycling may be driven by both extrinsic and intrinsic motivations, waste reduction is fundamentally driven by intrinsic motivations. So that, as social norms may well be effective for increasing recycling insofar as recycling entails more reciprocity and visibility related to individual actions, they might not be adequate for actions aimed at reducing waste, which often lack a social and relational component.

When individual motivations are considered, traditional policy tools typically considered, as Pigouviav taxes (that is pricing proportional to the externality or waste pressures), necessitate deeper pondering.

Actually, as already emphasized in the previous section, people responding to intrinsic motivations are less interested in external monetary incentives. On the contrary, the introduction of a monetary incentive might actually crowd-out the intrinsic motivation at the basis of waste-related behaviours. This crowding-out effect might increase if people perceive a control on their activity (Frey and Jegen 2001; Bowles and Polania-Reyes 2012), and a crowding-in effect might prevail if the monetary incentive is considerably higher than the value people confer on their activity (Bolle and Otto 2010). On the other hand, external non-monetary interventions could crowd-in intrinsic motivations by supporting individuals' perceived competences and sense of autonomy in carrying out particular activities aimed at waste management. The introduction of monetary incentives should be considered very carefully, especially when dealing with actions aimed at waste reduction, which is mainly a hidden behaviour. In fact, pecuniary incentives might trigger individuals who are not spontaneously driven by intrinsic motivations but at the same time it might crowd-out intrinsic motivations determining a loss of participation from those already acting to reduce waste. As in Gneezy and Rustichini (2000b), a sort of justification effect can arise to mitigate people's guilt: since a payment is expected based on the waste generated, people may not feel guilty if their waste increases. In this case, the introduction of an economic incentive could have a negative net result on waste reduction.

Also for what concerns extrinsic motivations as drivers of the more visible recycling behaviour, pecuniary spurs must be carefully considered. Actually, high monetary incentives might crowd-out motivation effects, when the action is visible. High economic incentives do not allow individuals to demonstrate to society that their performance of an activity is for reasons other than pecuniary ones (Thøgersen 2003; Bènabou and Tirole 2006). On the other hand, if the action is hidden, a crowding-in effect should prevail (Ariely et al. 2009). When action is visible, extrinsic motivation may be incentivized by any action that facilitates the visibility of the effort.[7]

2.3.1   How to Capture Intrinsic and Extrinsic Motivation in the Waste Realm

Empirical analysis about waste management has considered different kinds of variable to capture and measure individual motivations. Micro-level data on personal attitudes towards the environment are generally adopted to understand the influence of intrinsic and extrinsic motivations on waste-related behaviours.

Intrinsic motivations are often measured through proxies about individuals' environmental values (Barr 2007) and concerns for the environment (Ebreo and Vining 2001). In Viscusi et al. (2011), for instance, warm-glow is captured by the answers to specific questions on whether the respondent considers herself as being an environmentalist and dummy variable for whether the respondent would be upset with neighbours if they do not recycle. Similarly, Czajkowski et al. (2017) elicit moral or intrinsic norms through specific attitudinal questions made in ad hoc questionnaire measuring the degree of satisfaction respondents perceive from recycling at home by themselves, or if they consider the behaviour as a moral or ethical duty. The calculation of the Green Moral Index (a measure of intrinsic motivations) by Berglund (2006) is based on the replies about respondents' motivations

---

[7]Abbott et al. (2013) consider curbside collection as one way to facilitate the visibility of recycling efforts.

of sorting to the statements: 'I want to think of myself as a responsible person'; 'I should do what I want others to do'; 'I want to contribute to a better environment'; 'it is economical for the society at large'. In D'Amato et al. (2016), whose analysis uses data from the Survey of Public Attitudes and Behaviours toward the Environment, conducted in England in 2009, individual environmental values which are used to measure individual warm-glow are captured by respondents' degree of consciousness about the potential impacts of food production and disposal and by the individuals' perception of their contribution to help the environment. A different kind of proxy for intrinsic motivations is proposed by Cecere et al. (2014), whose empirical investigation is based on individual data collected in 2011 by the Gallup Organization on behalf of Eurobarometer (EU Commission). On the basis of their theoretical model, individuals' intrinsic motivations are captured by the extent to which individuals prefer not to pay taxes according to the quantity of waste by themselves generated but, rather, to pay taxes for the waste management of the community, independently from their own production.[8] In this case, the authors consider that people responding to intrinsic motivations are not interested in external incentives, either positive (rewards) or negative (fines), as a Pigouvian tax, but are more interested in funding public goods as public infrastructure, which clearly relates to more altruistic preferences.

Measures of extrinsic motivations mainly concern social norm and peer pressure. Czajkowski et al. (2017), for instance, measure social pressure through direct questions about respondents' beliefs about neighbours' judgments on their recycling behaviours.[9] In similar fashion, the external social norm component is captured in Viscusi et al. (2011) by a dummy variable for whether the respondent's neighbours would be upset if they noticed someone who do not recycle. In D'Amato et al. (2016), instead, the individual perception of the social norm is caught by the respondents' degree of agreement with the statement 'People have a duty to recycle'. Differently from the others, Cecere et al. (2014) use

---

[8]The former, pricing waste according to effective production, is more Pigouvian in style. The latter inclines more towards cost recovery strategies, funding public infrastructure (e.g. drop off recycling centres) that supports composting, recycling, and proper disposal through waste taxes or tariffs.

[9]The dataset to capture extrinsic motivations is the same used for measures about intrinsic motivations, and this holds for all the other papers that are considered in this subsection.

proxies to measure extrinsic motivations so that to capture the two main characteristics of behaviours driven by these kinds of motivations, that is: to be *socially* recognized as 'environmentally friendly', and to be *visible* to others. To this purpose, the behaviours they consider are mainly associated to the activity of buying,[10] which is a visible action, at least to the seller, to other purchasers and to friends.

Differently from the above-mentioned studies, Abbot et al. (2013) do not consider the use of surveys, but panel data of 317 English local authorities (period 2006–2008) on household recycling volume and determinants. On the basis of their theoretical model, the warm-glow effect is measured as the time devoted to recycling due to an improvement in curbside provision, which, without the warm-glow effect, should instead lead to a cut down of time, through the efficiency effect. Social norm is instead defined as the mean recycling volume of a reference group and measures the responsiveness of the recycling volume of a particular observed element to its reference.

2.3.2   Complementarity and Substitutability Relationship Between Waste Management Behaviours

As emphasized above, the two waste-related behaviours are different and are spurred by the two kinds of motivations, extrinsic and intrinsic, in different ways. In this situation, individuals' choices on the levels of each effort might both strengthen and weaken the other effort. In fact, since both behaviours are costly, individuals will choose the combination that maximizes their net returns. Hence, for instance, if individuals' pro-environmental behaviours are triggered mainly by extrinsic motivations, that is, by the desire to obtain social approval, they will be more likely to expend higher levels of effort on more visible actions.

The analysis of potential interrelationships between waste management behaviours may be of great interest, since, by admitting the possibility that recycling and reduction efforts may complement or substitute in individuals' preferences, it is possible to consider additional potential channels through which policies and behavioural drivers can affect the different dimensions characterizing waste-related behaviours.

---

[10] Recycled products or products with low environmental impact, which are *socially* considered as environmentally friendly.

Two opposite situations may arise. On the one hand, incentives and facilities to encourage one waste management behaviour may have positive effects on the other behaviour too, by stimulating a pro-environmental lifestyle and by affecting people's cultural learning of new preferences (Bowles and Polania-Reyes 2012). On the other hand, a substitutability relationship may exist due to a multi-tasking effect à la Holmstrom and Milgrom (1991), where the individual devotes less effort to the waste behaviour less incentivized (or less condemned) by policies, since it lacks any formal incentive compared to the other effort. In the European countries, where stronger incentives have been devoted towards increasing recycling than towards waste minimization,[11] if a relationship of substitutability exists, a sort of trade-off between the two pro-environmental activities may emerge, so that individuals might feel some obligation to recycle but none to consider reducing their waste. Catlin and Wang (2013) show that the option of recycling may even induce an increase in waste production by mitigating the guilt associated with wasteful consumption. However, in their study, the substitutability relationship between waste reduction and recycling is implicitly proposed with respect to specific kinds of product, as office papers or restroom paper hand towels.[12] Substitutability and complementarity relationships between waste behaviours in a more general setting have been deeply investigated in D'Amato et al. (2016) both theoretically and empirically. The impact of policy and behavioural factors, as warm-glow and social norm, on waste recycling and reduction efforts are analysed, considering that the two efforts may interact in the individual utility function. Their empirical analysis[13] adopts structural equation modelling (SEM), particularly suited for testing complementarity/substitutability relationships between waste reduction and recycling, given the possibility that this technique offers estimation of both the direct and indirect effects among the involved variables. The results show that the two waste behaviours

[11] Between 2001 and 2011, recycling and composting of municipal waste increased from 27 to 40% in the EU-27, while landfilling decreased from 56 to 37% (Eurostat 2013). Only 11 countries cut their generation of municipal waste per capita, whilst 21 countries increased their production (EEA 2013).

[12] The products used in their lab and field experiments consider materials that are used in the workplace or other environments and for which the consumers do not directly pay.

[13] Data from the Survey of Public Attitudes and Behaviors Toward the Environment, conducted in England in 2009.

reinforce each other, revealing that a complementarity relationship exists. The different outcome from Catlin and Wang (2013) may be due to the wider dimension that recycling and reduction behaviours assume in their analysis, not limited to choices over specific products, but over a plurality of items. In this more general setting it is conceivable that people motivated to recycle show high sensibility towards waste problems and waste reduction. Given the complementarity relationship between the two waste behaviours, the analysis of total effects reveals that policies oriented at improving recycling have also an indirect positive effect on waste reduction, even if their impact is quite low, however less than the impact induced by warm-glow. Even if the two waste behaviours are complements, intrinsic motivations that induce waste reduction ask for deeper policy interventions than the ones which simply reduce the opportunity cost of recycling.

2.4   FIELD EVIDENCE ON WASTE BEHAVIOUR

In the highlighted behavioural perspective field experiment method which, differently from laboratory method, considers the participants' natural everyday environment, appears to be a powerful tool for policy-makers to better understand how to properly design a policy[14] that effectively incentivizes individuals towards waste reduction and recycling. The aim of this section is to analyse some field experiments that can contribute to a better understanding of the motivations that lead individuals to adopt a pro-social behaviour in the waste realm.[15]

Some field experiments have tested to what extent external monetary incentives affect recycling and waste reduction behaviours, with puzzling results. Fullerton and Kinnaman (1996), for instance, in their natural field experiment, estimate the effect of a 'pricing by the bag' programme on the weight of the garbage, the number of containers, the weight per can and the amount of recycling of 75 households in Charlottesville, United States. Their aim is to investigate if the introduction of a price per bag of garbage affects the volume and the weight of

---

[14]The policy may also include nudges, that is 'any aspect of the choice architecture that alters people's behaviour in a predictable way without forbidding any options or significantly changing their economic incentives' (Thaler and Sunstein 2008, p. 6).

[15]List (2011) underlines how field experiment can be used to enhance economics understanding on economics theory and facts.

the garbage, as well as the number of bags. Furthermore, they are also interested in how the tariff influences the rate of recycling, which still remains a free option. Even though the pricing programme does not set any private reward, we can think of this as the saving in the cost of an additional bag of garbage. The author measured the weight and the number of containers as well as the amount of recycled waste a month before and a month after the introduction of the regulation and found some interesting results: first, after the introduction of the policy the average households reduced the garbage weight by only 14% and the volume by 37% with respect to the situation prior to the programme; second, the weight of the recycled material increased by only 16%.[16] These positive results are, nevertheless counterbalanced by the negative indirect effects that the authors detect about additional illegal dumping that account for 28–43% of the reduction of garbage, whose true reduction is hence only 10%.

Perplexing results about the impact of monetary incentives on recycling are also found in Koford et al. (2012), whose results about intrinsic motivations at the basis of recycling behaviour are instead more intriguing. The authors investigate how households' recycling responds to different incentives, such as monetary incentives and communication appeals. On a sample of 256 households, they combine 3 monetary incentives (0$, 1$, 2$) with 4 different communication appeals: the first one only reporting facts about recycling (Informative appeal); the second one displaying a threatening message on the damage that not recycling causes to the environment (Guilt appeal); the third one showing uses of the recycled material with a positive social impact (Feel good appeal). The last communication appeal is no communication. Before the experiment, households recycling habits have been monitored for one month. Results show that the highest amount of recycled material is provided by the group that received the 1$/no communication treatment, whilst the lowest is provided by the group that received the 1$/informative treatment. The low level of pecuniary incentives (1$), which is moreover given independently from the amount recycled, does not allow to draw

---

[16]Controlling for the socio-economic characteristics of the sample in a regression model, they also found that the decrease in garbage is greater for high income households while stomping (i.e. the practice to stuff more garbage as possible in a single bag) is greater for married couples.

straight conclusions on the efficacy of monetary drivers. More interesting results come, instead, from a time series model, which show that informative and feel good appeal have a positive impact whilst guilt appeal appears to be detrimental to recycling. Increasing one's own knowledge on recycling fosters the adoption of the behaviour. Moreover, showing how recycled material can be practically reused can have the same effect, because the individual can acknowledge that she can actually contribute to something bigger. In other words, information as well as a positive feedback on the results helps individual to translate their intention to have a more environmental-friendly behaviour into action (Thaler and Sunstein 2008).

On the possible crowding-out effect of external incentives on intrinsic motivations, Rommel et al. (2015) show some interesting results. They test if intrinsic motivation to avoid garbage is crowded out by introducing monitoring and small rewards and show that the crowding-out effect depends on the way the incentive is framed, i.e. it depends on whether the external incentive is perceived as creating a monetary reward (controlling function) or a social reward (supporting function), as concluded also in Heyman and Ariely (2004). Rommel and colleagues study if increasing the level of external intervention increases the adoption of the no junk mail stickers on households' mailboxes. They apply four 'progressive' treatments: in the first one, only the stickers were provided; in the second one, they added a message explaining that 30 kg of paper per mailbox could be saved each year; in the third one they further pointed out that in approximately 2 weeks the distributors would return to see if the sticker had been attached to the mailbox; the final one added that if a sticker was found, the mailbox owner would have received a symbolic gift. The findings show that increasing the level of intervention actually increases the use of stickers and that the effect of a reward is to increase the use of sticker by 12% with respect to the baseline (only stickers). The authors conclude that the positive crowding-in effect might be largely due to the way the intervention was set, through the combination of a social reward with a supportive framing.

The effectiveness of social norms as well have been investigated using field experiment settings to verify their effects on waste-related behaviours. Kallbekken and Sælen (2013), set up an experiment on a sample of hotel guests with the aim of testing the effectiveness of two treatments in reducing food waste generation. The first one is based on the scientific discovery that reducing the size of the plate actually reduces the food intake and therefore might reduce the correlated waste. In the second treatment they also displayed a message at the buffet table to encourage guests to help themselves more than once, in order to make it a socially salient norm. It is expected that guests will load their plate less if they feel allowed to go back to the buffet and load the plate again. Findings estimated both interventions reduce food waste. It is interesting to highlight that in this specific setting food waste reduction is a visible action and, in line with the reasoning carried out in the previous sections, is positively affected by social norm.

Social norms and peer comparison have also been shown to be effective in stimulating waste recycling, as for Milford et al. (2015), with a natural field experiment conducted on household waste in Kristiansand, Norway. The treatment consists of personal letters to households in Kristiansand with information about own waste data and corresponding waste data in a comparison group. Besides the control group two other treatment groups are considered. The first one concerns total households' waste generation, and the second one concerns households' degree of recycling. Whilst the effects on waste reduction of the information letters are not clear, the effects on recycling are extremely positive, with an increase of 2% points among households that received the letters than among households in the control group. Moreover, even if the effect is stronger for households with a level of recycling lower than the median of the comparison group, also households above the median increase their recycling. No undesirable 'boomerang effect' (Shultz et al. 2007) was hence detected, that can instead be one of the problems when considering social descriptive norms that people do not want to deviate. Since being deviant is both below and above the norm, people whose behaviour is above could be induced to reduce their targets. This problem may be so relevant that Cialdini (2003), gives particular emphasis to the importance of considering both injunctive and descriptive norms to motivate pro-environmental action.[17]

---

[17]More specifically, the injunctive norm entails 'perceptions of which behaviors are typically approved or disapproved' (Cialdini 2003, p. 105), while the descriptive norm entails 'perceptions of which behaviors are typically performed' (Cialdini 2003, p. 105).

2.5   Conclusions

This chapter highlights the need to tackle the challenges related to waste management with the awareness of the role played by people's preferences and attitudes. We specifically address the role of intrinsic and extrinsic motivations related to the two waste-related behaviours: reduction and recycling. Several studies point out that the two actions are different and may be steered by the two kinds of motivations in diverse ways. More specifically, the more visible action recycling is driven by both intrinsic and extrinsic motivations, whilst the less visible waste minimization is mainly driven by intrinsic motivations.

In this perspective, policy interventions in the waste management realm should respond both to consumers' reactions to economic incentives and to the different recycling and waste reduction responses induced by different motivations, considering also the potential interrelationships between the two behaviours. Increasing people's awareness about waste problem, through well-designed information and educational campaign is a need that governments should consider to achieve long-term sustainability targets.

References

Abbott, A., Nandeibam, S., & O'Shea, L. (2013). Recycling: Social norms and warm-glow revisited. *Ecological Economics, 90*, 10–18.

Andreoni, J. (1989). Giving with impure altruism: Applications to charity and Ricardian equivalence. *Journal of Political Economy, 97*(6), 1447–1458.

Andreoni, J. (1990). Impure altruism and donations to public goods: A theory of warm-glow giving? *Economic Journal, 100*(401), 464–477.

Ariely, D., Bracha, A., & Meier, S. (2009). Doing good or doing well? Image motivation and monetary incentives in behaving prosocially. *The American Economic Review, 99*, 544–555.

Barr, S. (2007). Factors influencing environmental attitudes and behaviors: A U.K. case study of household waste management. *Environment and Behavior, 39*(4), 435–473.

Becker, G. S. (1974). A theory of social interactions. *Journal of Political Economy, 82*, 1063–1093.

Bénabou, R., & Tirole, J. (2006). Incentives and prosocial behavior. *American Economic Review, 96*(5), 1652–1678.

Berglund, C. (2006). The assessment of households' recycling costs: The role of personal motives. *Ecological Economics, 56*, 560–569.

Bolle, F., & Otto, P. E. (2010). A price is a signal: On intrinsic motivation, crowding-out, and crowding-in. *Kyklos, 63*, 9–22.

Bortoleto, A. P. (2014). *Waste prevention policy and behaviour: New approaches to reducing waste generation and its environmental impacts.* London and New York: Routledge.

Bowles, S., & Polania-Reyes, S. (2012). Economic incentives and social preferences: Substitutes or complements? *Journal of Economic Literature, 50*(2), 368–425.

Brekke, K. A., Kipperberg, G., & Nyborg, K. (2010). Social interaction in responsibility ascription: The case of household recycling. *Land Economics, 86*, 766–784.

Brekke, K. A., Kverndokk, S., & Nyborg, K. (2003). An economic model of moral motivation. *Journal of Public Economics, 87*, 1967–1983.

Catlin, J. R., & Wang, Y. (2013). Recycling gone bad: When the option to recycle increases resource consumption. *Journal of Consumer Psychology, 23*(1), 122–127.

Cecere, G., Mancinelli, S., & Mazzanti, M. (2014). Waste prevention and social preferences: The role of intrinsic and extrinsic motivations. *Ecological Economics, 107*, 163–176.

Cialdini, R. B. (2003). Crafting normative messages to protect the environment. *Current Directions in Psychological Science, 12*(4), 105–109.

Czajkowski, M., Hanley, N., & Nyborg, K. (2017). Social norms, morals and self-interest as determinants of pro-environment behaviours: The case of household recycling. *Environmental & Resource Economics, 66*(4), 647–670.

D'Amato, A., Mancinelli, S., & Zoli, M. (2016). Complementarity vs substitutability in waste management behaviors. *Ecological Economics, 123*, 84–94.

Deci, E. L. (1971). Effects of externally mediated rewards on intrinsic motivation. *Journal of Personality and Social Psychology, 18*(1), 105–115.

Deci, E. L. (1975). *Intrinsic motivation.* New York: Plenum Press.

Ebreo, A., & Vining, J. (2001). How similar are recycling and waste reduction? Future orientation and reasons for reducing waste as predictors of self-reported behavior. *Environment and Behavior, 33*(3), 424–448.

EEA. (2013). *Managing municipal solid waste—A review of achievements in 32 European countries* (EEA Report No. 2/2013). European Environmental Agency, Copenhagen.

Eurostat. (2013). Newsrelease (33/2013–4 March 2013).

Fehr, E., & Gächter, S. (2000). Fairness and retaliation: The economics of reciprocity. *Journal of Economic Perspectives, 14*(3), 159–181.

Fehr, E., & Schmidt, K. (1999). A theory of fairness, competition, and cooperation. *Quarterly Journal of Economics, 114*(3), 817–868.

Frey, B. S., Goette, L. (1999). *Does pay motivate volunteers?*, Mimeo, Institute for Empirical Research in Economics, University of Zurich.

Frey, B. S., & Jegen R. (2001). Motivation crowding theory: A survey of empirical evidence. *Journal of Economic Surveys, 5*(5), 589–611.

Fullerton, D., & Kinnaman, T. (1996). Household responses to pricing garbage by the bag. *American Economic Review, 86*(4), 971–984.

Gneezy, U., & Rustichini, A. (2000a). Pay enough or don't pay at all. *Quarterly Journal of Economics, 115*(3), 791–810.

Gneezy, U., & Rustichini, A. (2000b). A fine is a price. *Journal of Legal Studies, 29*(1), 1–18.

Gneezy, U., Meier, S., & Rey-Biel, P. (2011). When and why incentives (don't) work to modify behavior. *Journal of Economic Perspectives, 25*(4), 191–210.

Hage, O., Söderholm, P., & Berglund, C. (2009). Norms and economic motivation in household recycling: Empirical evidence from Sweden. *Resource and Conservation Policy, 53,* 155–165.

Halvorsen, B. (2008). Effects of norms and opportunity cost of time on household recycling. *Land Economics, 84,* 501–516.

Heyman, J., & Ariely, D. (2004). Effort for payment—A tale of two markets. *Psychological Science, 15*(11), 787–793.

Holmstrom, B., & Milgrom, P. (1991). Multitask principal-agent analyses: Incentive contracts, asset ownership, and job design. *Journal of Law Economics and Organization, 7,* 24–52.

Kallbekken, S., & Sælen, H. (2013). "Nudging" hotel guests to reduce food waste as a win–win environmental measure. *Economics Letters, 119*(3), 325–327.

Kesternich, M., Reif, C., & Rübbelke, D. (2017). Recent trends in behavioral environmental economics. *Environmental & Resource Economics, 67*(3), 403–411.

Kinnaman, T. (2006). Examining the justification for residential recycling. *Journal of Economic Perspectives, 20*(4), 219–232.

Koford, B. C., Blomquist, G. C., Hardesty, D. M., & Troske, K. R. (2012). Estimating consumer willingness to supply and willingness to pay for curbside recycling. *Land Economics, 88*(4), 745–763.

List, J. A. (2011). Why economists should conduct field experiments and 14 tips for pulling one off. *The Journal of Economic Perspectives, 25*(3), 3–15.

Meier, S. (2007). A survey on economic theories and field evidence on pro-social behavior. In B. S. Frey & A. Stutzer (Eds.), *Economics and psychology: A promising new cross-disciplinary field* (pp. 51–88). Cambridge: MIT Press.

Milford, A. B., Øvrum, A., & Helgesen, H. (2015). *Nudges to increase recycling and reduce waste.* Discussion Paper, Norwegian Agricultural Economics Research Institute.

Olson, M. (1965). *The logic of collective action: Public goods and the theory of groups.* Cambridge: Harvard University Press.

Rabin, M. (1993). Incorporating fairness into game theory and economics. *American Economic Review, 83*(5), 1281–1302.

Rommel, J., Buttmann, V., Liebig, G., Schoenwetter, S., & Svart-Groeger, V. (2015). Motivation crowding theory and pro-environmental behavior: Experimental evidence. *Economics Letters, 129,* 42–44.

Schultz, P. W., Nolan, J. M., Cialdini, R. B., Goldstein, N. J., & Griskevicius, V. (2007). The constructive, destructive, and reconstructive power of social norms. *Psychological Science, 18*(5), 429–434.

Thaler, R., & Sunstein, C. (2008). *Nudge: The gentle power of choice architecture.* New Haven, Conn: Yale.

Thørgersen, J. (2003). Monetary incentives and recycling: Behavioural and psychological reactions to a performance-dependent garbage fee. *Journal of Consumer Policy, 26,* 197–228.

Titmuss, R. M. (1970). *The gift relationship.* London: Allen and Unwin.

Viscusi, W. K., Huber, J., & Bell, J. (2011). Promoting recycling: Private values, social norms, and economic incentives. *American Economic Review, 101*(3), 65–70.

CHAPTER 3

Waste Policies and Individual Behaviours

Abstract This chapter investigates waste policies that may affect individuals' behaviour towards waste minimization and recycling. Both market base mechanisms, as unit-based pricing for unsorted waste, and technical policies, as adoption of curbside or drop-off systems are considered. The strength and weakness of each mechanism as drivers of people's waste-related behaviours are highlighted.

Keywords Waste minimizing · Recycling · Waste-related behaviours
Waste policies

3.1 Introduction

This chapter expands and complements Chapter 2 in several directions. Firstly, we account for the role of different recycling policies and their effect on recycling performances. In particular, we focus both on market base mechanisms, such as unit-based pricing for unsorted waste, and on technical policies, like the adoption and diffusion of curbside (or door-to-door) collection, drop-off systems and civic amenities. In doing so, we focus on the possible interactions between policy efficacy and consumer behaviour. Just to give a quick example, it is reasonable to assume that if drop-off systems are distant from households' living space or are often full, their efficacy is expected to be fairly low. However, highly intrinsically motivated households might still want to bear the cost of travelling to the nearest recycling centre because of the warm-glow they obtain from the pro-environmental behaviour. On the contrary, if drop-off systems are often full of garbage or are, more generally, not collected frequently enough generating bad smells and negative impact on the closest neighbourhoods, citizens with low intrinsic motivations might have a further lower incentive to recycle. Finally, some negative interactions might occur in municipalities which adopt more than one recycling policies, as door-to-door might cannibalize the expected return of drop-off systems and vice versa.

Secondly, we move our attention towards the less studied but extremely relevant topic of waste prevention and/or minimization. Also in this case, our focus is on the possible interactions between policy instruments, individual motivation and socio-economic context. The efficacy of minimization policy depends indeed on both the convenience of the policy itself (how simple it is for the consumer to respect the prescribed behaviour) and on the several socio-economic and behavioural aspects. Just to give a simple example, even if older people have enough free time to spend in reuse and repair activities, the implementation of an online-based flea market might result ineffective in incentivizing this segment of population towards prevention behaviour.

Finally, we highlight the role and the importance of other relevant policies such as specific knowledge and information policies, and their interaction with recycling and minimization instruments. The intuition also in this case is very straightforward. Separating waste at home might be tedious and difficult, as it is often hard to understand how to correctly separate the packaging of different food. A good information policy can help families to understand, for instance, where to throw the internal and external packaging of crackers; or what to do with old batteries and medicines. All these information, in the end, help to have a higher quality separate collection fraction, with a lower reject rates and an overall better environmental output. Specific knowledge, on the contrary, act on two different levels. On the one hand, a higher level of knowledge is a direct result of good information policies, and can improve recycling performances thanks to the simple mechanism explained a few lines above. On the other hand, and more importantly, specific knowledge can help in shaping citizens' environmental awareness and increasing their overall interest in waste and, more generally, environmental issues.

The chapter is structured as follows: Sect. 3.2 focuses on recycling policies and their interaction with individual motivation; Sect. 3.3 focuses on prevention and minimization, whilst Sect. 3.4 concludes.

3.2   RECYCLING POLICIES

The role of households' behaviours with respect to separate collection is a fundamental precondition to the success of the evolution towards a 'recycling society'. Besides individual motivations (which have been investigated in Chapter 2), it is commonly acknowledged in the economic literature (e.g. Guagnano et al. 1994; Abbott et al. 2013; Beatty et al. 2007) that better recycling policies that increase provisions of appropriate services and/or implement waste disposal fees positively influence household participation in waste sorting.[1] The intuition behind this statement is fairly straightforward: households' recycling effort is characterized by high time opportunity costs and, often, a big effort. As a consequence, any policy that makes recycling more convenient should increase the participation of households in a correct waste management system (Sidique et al. 2010). In this perspective, two kinds of policies may be considered as affecting costs: unit pricing programmes and improvements to convenience factors such as the proximity of drop-off centres. In the first case, the relative price of recycling with respect to residual waste is influenced. In the second case, the opportunity costs of recycling in terms of time spent by households are of concern.

With unit pricing programmes, which charge residents for the quantity of unsorted waste, positive incentives on recycling efforts can be induced by increasing households' costs of discarding additional waste relative to the cost of recycling. The literature provides empirical evidence of that result. For example, Hong et al. (1993), using a large sample of households from the metropolitan area of Portland, Oregon, show that a unit increase in the fee increases the amount of recycling. This result is robust to several specifications. Hong (1999), exploiting a rich data set which includes 3017 Korean households, finds that a rise in waste collection fee induces households to recycle more wastes. However, he also shows that after a certain threshold, unit base pricing alone is not capable of incentivizing recycling unless the tax is coupled

---

[1]Following Dahlén et al. (2007) regarding the phrase waste sorting, we intend household activities towards the separate disposal of waste materials.

by alternative waste policies like more frequent recyclable pickup services. Ferrara and Missios (2005) using micro-data from Ontario, in Canada, found that both waste policies like mandatory recycling programmes and unit-based pricing have significant impacts on recycling levels. Kipperberg (2007) finds that a disposal fee provides a significant economic incentive to Norwegian households. However, other studies have not obtained the same results. Fullerton and Kinnaman (1996), for instance, investigated the impact of unit pricing directly measuring the weight and volume of garbage for 75 US households before and after the implementation of a user fee programme. Their study shows that households reduced the number of bags used for recycling, but not necessarily the actual weight of their garbage. Moreover, the authors highlight that unit pricing might also possibly increase illegal dumping. Kinnaman and Fullerton (2000), in a complementary study on the US, show that 'the implementation of a $1 user fee could decrease the quantity of garbage by 412 pounds per person per year but increase recycling by only 30 pounds per person per year' (Page 441). However, they stress that the extra garbage is likely to be disposed thanks to illegal dumping or bury activities. Summarizing, this literature is still rather controversial and not completely capable of producing a consolidated result. These different outcomes can be justified by recognizing that unit pricing only provides an indirect incentive to recycling (Jenkins et al. 2003).[2] Dahlén et al. (2007) highlight the possibility that unit pricing programmes worsen the quality of recycling by inducing people to collect residual waste in inappropriate places at the drop-off centres for recyclables. Moreover, Reschovsky and Stone (1994) have identified some concerns regarding unit pricing schemes that are related, for example, to potential incentives to illegal dumping, high administrative costs and the regressive impact that variable fees can have on low-income residents. All these factors may explain the low popularity of unit pricing schemes. In Italy, where our empirical analysis is undertaken (in Chapter 5), unit pricing schemes have been implemented only in some hundreds of municipalities, mostly in the northern part of the country (EC 2015).[3] Similarly, these schemes have been adopted in moderation by EU Member States, where the

---

[2] An accurate review of existing empirical studies that explore the impacts of unit pricing and curbside recycling policies on household recycling efforts is reported in Jenkins et al. (2003).

[3] In Italy, there are approximately 8000 municipalities as of 2017.

main source of financing waste collection and disposal costs is through flat charges or municipal taxes that are unrelated to the amount of generated waste.

Policies may also provide services that reduce the time and effort spent by households in their waste management activities. Some studies (e.g. Sidique et al. 2010; Saphores et al. 2006; Dahlén et al. 2007; Ando and Gosselin 2005; Folz 1999) have emphasized how nearness to a recycling centre can positively influence waste sorting behaviours. Regarding this aspect, two recycling programmes deserve consideration: drop-off[4] and curbside. The implementation of a local drop-off scheme for collecting specific recycling materials reduces the time and effort spent by individuals to store and transport those materials and, as a consequence, should increase their sorting behaviour. In that perspective, introducing a curbside recycling programme makes household recycling even more convenient. Among the earliest works in this field, Jenkins et al. (2003), for instance, using survey data demonstrate that the presence of curbside collection increases significantly the probability that a given material is recycled. In a similar work, Reschovsky and Stone (1994) find that curbside programmes can significantly increase recycling rates, especially if implemented in conjunction with compulsory recycling targets and unit-based pricing. However, curbside collection schemes have some unfavourable aspects. They occupy space on householders' properties (Larsen et al. 2010) and are costly policies, and their marginal impact on total recycled quantities is not very relevant because they can cannibalize returns from drop-off recycling centres (Beatty et al. 2007). On the other hand, drop-off recycling programmes are less costly policies (Sidique et al. 2010) because the transportation costs are relocated to the recyclers. Regarding drop-off centres, some details are worth noting. In most EU countries, municipalities have generally adopted two types of drop-off systems: bring sites and Civic Amenities (CA). Bring sites are recycling centres that are often located in strategic places across neighbourhoods such as small squares or large streets. Their efficacies can be high, including in those municipalities with curbside systems, especially when collections do not occur too often. In several European cities, for example, curbside systems operate once a week, and large families

---

[4]'Drop-off recycling is a recycling program where designated sites are established to collect a range of recyclables and usually recyclers themselves are required to deposit the sorted recyclables in specially marked containers' (Sidique et al. 2010, p. 163).

living in small flats face the problem of storing waste before collection. A nearby bring site collection point can operate in that way. The role of Civic Amenity sites is very different. They are collection points for a whole set of recyclable materials and are located often at one or a few points just outside city centres. The main advantage of that service is that CA sites generally contain a plethora of collection bins, into which households can throw several different types of materials that are often more difficult to separately collect at home. This is often the case for medicines, batteries, waste electronic equipment (WEEE) and exhaust oil, for example. In other terms, the aim of the second tool is to obtain a higher quality separate collection system rather than making separate collection easier. In summary, from the literature reported above, an apparent trade-off exists between curbside and drop-off recycling systems: the opportunity costs that must be borne by households (in terms of time) and the costs that must be borne by municipalities.

The efforts devoted by households to waste sorting may be influenced by other kinds of policies such as specific knowledge and frequency of recyclables collection (often called 'convenience' in this literature). Information policies about how and where to separately collect recyclable materials implies time savings by people and has been already recognized as a relevant factor in their involvement with recycling (Barr 2007; Gamba and Oskamp 1994; Hornik et al. 1995; Vining and Ebreo 1990). Sideque et al. (2010), in a study on the Lansing area in Michigan, show, among other things, as drop-off sites tend to be more successful when recyclers feel that recycling activities are convenient and when they are familiar with the site. The importance of 'convenience' is also a key result of the work by Saphores et al. (2006), which studies the determinants of waste recycling using a mail survey of 3000 California households. Interestingly, they found that the effect of convenience and information policies is mediated by the age of the respondents. Information programmes, for instance, should target teenagers or young adults, as most adults between 36 and 65 years old are more sensitive to environmental issues because they grew up with the environmental movement (in northern California). Convenience, on the other side, is a key aspect of a successful separate collection scheme which targets older adults. Folz (1999) stresses as mandatory targets and the convenience of same-day pick-up of recyclables, were the main factors influencing high recycling performances in the 1990s for US cities. Moreover, concerning collection frequency, Abbott et al. (2011) showed that recycling rate increase with lower frequencies of residual waste collection. Moreover, recycling behaviour should be encouraged by high frequencies of recyclables collection (Kirakozian 2016).

3.3   PREVENTION

3.3.1   Prevention Policies

In this paragraph we will quickly present some examples of prevention and minimization policies. We believe this is a necessary step, because, differently from recycling policies—which are well known and consolidated in literature—prevention and minimization policies are less known and still understudied.

With waste prevention policies, we generally mean a set of instruments with the precise aim of reducing wastes generated by a given group of people, being it in regions, municipalities or countries. Generally, waste prevention programmes target specific waste streams and may include or not some precise objective of actual waste reduction (for instance, a 20% reduction in plastic waste). A common approach adopted by several countries is the creation of national guidelines with the aim of creating a shared framework on the topic. The NRWF Household Waste Prevention Toolkit implemented in the UK in 2004 is a valid example of this approach, as it represents a series of specific indications on how waste prevention plans should be structured in the UK (DEFRA 2009). A similar approach has been undertaken by the European Commission, which has proposed a series of guidelines for waste prevention, aiming at clarifying 'the main concepts related to waste prevention, suggesting a framework to develop Waste Prevention Programmes and providing best practices and examples of national and regional programmes employing an effective mix of measures' (see: http://ec.europa.eu/environment/waste/prevention/guidelines.htm). It also includes a list of further materials on waste prevention theory and a list of best practices from all European countries. The creation of a guidance programme was a requirement of the 2008 Waste Framework Directive (Directive 2008/98/EC).

When it comes to specific examples of waste prevention programmes, the survey by Bortoleto (2015)[5] reports the two interesting cases of

---

[5] Chapter 3, pp. 41–47.

Austria and the UK. Austria enacted its Waste prevention and recycling strategy in 2007, a tool which was targeting five main areas of waste management, i.e. construction and demolition waste, industrial waste, household waste, food waste and repair and reuse. It is worth noticing the emphasis on repair and reuse, two fundamental aspects of the European waste framework directive. Without entering too much into details, for what concerns households waste, the Austrian plan includes a wide host of measures, like: internet fact sheet and best practices on prevention actions and prevention technologies; information campaign for households; consultants' support for families; incentive systems and donation schemes for food waste. For what concern repair and reuse, the programme helped to create a secondary market for equipment and furniture and promoted public campaign for supporting sustainable purchasing criteria. A national campaign on reuse was also introduced which had the aim of promoting an overall awareness on that topic, as well as establishing standards for second-hand shops (Bortoleto 2015). In line with the national principles, the city of Vienna, for instance, introduced three different prevention measures. Firstly, a web-based flea market, i.e. an online exchange platform for consumer goods and construction goods. Secondly, 23 local repair service centres (RUSZ) were created to promote repair service for electric households' appliances. Finally, the city lunched an information campaign to encourage individuals to spend money in service and culture instead of in the use of material goods.

A similar plan, called the Waste Prevention Program of England (DEFRA 2013) was launched in UK in 2013. Also this programme is in line with the Waste Framework Directive and has the purpose to reduce the total amount of waste generated by the country. The British plan differs slightly from the Austrian one as it targets more directly the industrial sector, aiming at including waste prevention into the design and the business model of manufacturing firms. Secondly, it seeks to promote repair and reuse, and tries to push firms to increase the life cycle of manufacturing goods. The plan applies to different materials and has specific recommendations for specific sectors. Just to give few examples, in the case of paper waste the programme recommends to improve and modify the design of goods in order to minimize their paper contents and to maximize the recycled content where possible. Moreover, a mandatory 5p purchase charge for plastic shopping bags has been imposed, with the aim to promote the use of biodegradable bags. An application of this prevention plan can be found, for instance, in the city of Manchester, which introduced a WEE reuse scheme that had the objective of repairing old electronic devices and diverting them from disposal. Similarly, in London, the Real nappies scheme provided a monetary incentive for the purchase of reusable nappies.

Similar programmes have been adopted also in Japan and France, just to mention some other examples. A good review can be found in Bortoleto (2015).

3.3.2   Prevention Policies and Individual Behaviour

Given the complex and varied nature of prevention policies it comes with no surprise that there are several possible interactions between human behaviour and policy effectiveness. Moreover, it must be noted that behaviour is only one of the elements which may positively or negatively interact with policy efficacy. Also, the socio-economic and physical contexts of the individual matter. Even more important, the impact that contextual factors have on policy efficacy may change from one policy to another. The ability to use a computer, often correlated with age, can have an important impact on the efficacy of an online-based flea market like the one introduced in Vienna, whilst it does not have any impact on the effectiveness of physical repair service centres. On the contrary, older people might have more free time to dedicate to reuse and repair activities. Reaching a good understanding of the socio-economic and physical contexts of households becomes, as a consequence, a crucial step in designing an effective waste prevention plan.

Obviously, this can also be a powerful tool in the hand of a policymaker, which can shape and design a prevention policy plan in the way that better suites its citizens (Todd and Gigerenzer 2012). In a deposit and refund scheme for glass bottle like, for instance, the one existing in Germany, this means being able to understand where to locate collection points and how to make them functional. What must be avoided, in such cases, are policies which generate confusion and give contrasting signals to consumers. Complex product labels or long product description on web sites are two typical sources of confusion, whilst prevention policies need to provide a clear signal without overloading consumers with too much information (Fasolo et al. 2007). As a consequence, a one-size-fit-all policy does not seem to be effective in the case of waste prevention and minimization, as the correct identification of all relevant contextual element is a necessary precondition for targeting minimization behaviour. Bortoleto (2015)[6] provides some interesting evidence in support of this idea. An important waste prevention decision, for instance, may regard the choice of buying or not vegetables wrapped in cellophane or other plastic materials. In this case, the contextual factors are: price, availability, real and perceived quality of the product, marketing strategies. Consumers who buy plastic- wrapped food are often moved by concerns on food quality, which is perceived to be higher in packaged food (Underwood and Klein 2002). Similarly, in absence on information on real product quality, consumers tend to prefer more expensive (and packaged) food, considering packaging as an indication of higher standard. Another example of how the context can influence the efficacy of a prevention policy, can be found in the case of home composting, whose efficacy depends on the availability of space for at home. Finally, the 'buy one get one free' type of offer can significantly increase the amount of food waste by pushing consumer to buy more food than they actually need (WRAP Report 2007). It is worth bearing in mind, that all these examples are material specific (and consequently shop-specific), and a comprehensive framework for waste prevention needs to account for all these specificities.

Another key factor for the success of these policies, as it was in the case of recycling, is the so-called convenience. With convenience we refer to how difficult and costly a given policy is for citizens. As mentioned above for the case of recycling, the success of a policy which implies households' involvement depends on the cost that these households have to bear in order to comply with this policy. Often, in waste management practices, effort means time, and convenience can in sense decrease the burden the households have to sustain. Moreover, it must be noted that households tend to a priori overestimate the level of discomfort of new waste practices, lobbying strongly against the approval of these schemes (Pieters 1991). A common example is volume based pay-as-you-through schemes, against which households tend to have several misperceptions of the actual cost and inconvenience level. Similarly, consumers can have a priori doubt on the quality of unpackaged or loosely packaged food (Bortoleto 2015). Similarly, in a study on refillable cosmetics, Lofthouse et al. (2007) show that consumers expect refills to be of lower quality with respect to packaged product. Finally, Tucker and Spiers (2003)

---

[6]See page 73.

highlight that prejudices and misconception hinder people participation to home composting, but these prejudices decreases through time after households become familiar with the new tool.

3.4   CONCLUSIONS

This chapter highlights the role of waste policies for both recycling and prevention. Regarding recycling, two kinds of policies may be considered as affecting costs: convenience factors and unit pricing programmes. If the first stream of literature is very consolidated, and show as an increase in convenience (for instance nearness to a recycling centre) can positively influence waste sorting behaviours, the same does not hold for the literature on the effect of unit pricing programmes. Similarly, also the literature on prevention and minimization highlights as convenience and context may influence the efficacy of several prevention programmes. Among the contextual factors, physical characteristics, spatial issue, availability, quality and economic cost of new actions are the main elements which might influence the efficacy of a minimization programme. Finally, specific knowledge and information policies capable of increasing the overall awareness of waste-related issues, appear to be two key aspects of both recycling and prevention policies.

REFERENCES

Abbott, A., Nandeibam, S., & O'Shea, L. (2011). Explaining the variation in household recycling rates across the UK. *Ecological Economics, 70*(11), 2214–2223.

Abbott, A., Nandeibam, S., & O'Shea, L. (2013). Recycling: Social norms and warm-glow revisited. *Ecological Economics, 90*, 10–18.

Ando, A. W., & Gosselin, A. Y. (2005). Recycling in multifamily dwellings: Does convenience matter? *Economic Inquiry, 43*(2), 426–438.

Barr, S. (2007). Factors influencing environmental attitudes and behaviors: A UK case study of household waste management. *Environment and Behavior, 39*(4), 435–473.

Beatty, T. K., Berck, P., & Shimshack, J. P. (2007). Curbside recycling in the presence of alternatives. *Economic Inquiry, 45*(4), 739–755.

Bortoleto, A. P. (2015). *Waste prevention policy and behaviour. New approaches to reducing waste generation and its environmental impacts*. New York: Routledge.

Dahlén, L., Vukicevic, S., Meijer, J. E., & Lagerkvist, A. (2007). Comparison of different collection systems for sorted household waste in Sweden. *Waste Management, 27*(10), 1298–1305.

DEFRA. (2009). Household waste prevention evidence review: L3m3-3(D)— Impact of household waste prevention interventions and campaigns. London.

DEFRA. (2013). *Waste prevention program for England, household waste prevention in action—Example from across England*. London: DEFRA.

European Commission. (2015). Country factsheet for South Italy. Support to member states in improving waste management based on assessment of member states' performance. Study conducted by Bipro, in cooperation with the Copenhagen Resource Institute. http://ec.europa.eu/environment/waste/framework/pdf/IT_SOUTH_factsheet_FINAL.pdf.

Fasolo, B., McClelland, G. H., & Todd, P. M. (2007). Escaping the tyranny of choice: When fewer attributes make choice easier. *Marketing Theory, 7*(1), 13–26.

Ferrara, I., & Missios, P. (2005). Recycling and waste diversion effectiveness: Evidence from Canada. *Environmental & Resource Economics, 30*(2), 221–238.

Folz, D. H. (1999). Municipal recycling performance: A public sector environmental success story. *Public Administration Review, 59*(4), 336–345.

Fullerton, D., & Kinnaman, T. C. (1996). Household responses to pricing garbage by the bag. *American Economic Review, 86*(4), 971–984.

Gamba, R. J., & Oskamp, S. (1994). Factors influencing community residents' participation in commingled curbside recycling programs. *Environment and Behavior, 26*(5), 587–612.

Guagnano, G. A., Dietz, T., & Stern, P. C. (1994). Willingness to pay for public goods: A test of the contribution model. *Psychological Science, 5*(6), 411–415.

Hong, S. (1999). The effects of unit pricing system upon household solid waste management: The Korean experience. *Journal of Environmental Management, 57*(1), 1–10.

Hong, S., Adams, R. M., & Love, H. A. (1993). An economic analysis of household recycling of solid wastes: The case of Portland, Oregon. *Journal of Environmental Economics and Management, 25*(2), 136–146.

Hornik, J., Cherian, J., Madansky, M., & Narayana, C. (1995). Determinants of recycling behavior: A synthesis of research results. *The Journal of Socio-Economics, 24*(1), 105–127.

Jenkins, R. R., Martinez, S. A., Palmer, K., & Podolsky, M. J. (2003). The determinants of household recycling: A material-specific analysis of recycling program features and unit pricing. *Journal of Environmental Economics and Management, 45*(2), 294–318.

Kinnaman, T. C., & Fullerton, D. (2000). Garbage and recycling with endogenous local policy. *Journal of Urban Economics, 48*(3), 419–442.

Kipperberg, G. (2007). A comparison of household recycling behaviors in Norway and the United States. *Environmental & Resource Economics, 36*(2), 215–235.

Kirakozian, A. (2016). The determinants of household recycling: Social influence, public policies and environmental preferences. *Applied Economics, 48*(16), 1481–1503.

Larsen, A. W., Merrild, H., Møller, J., & Christensen, T. H. (2010). Waste collection systems for recyclables: An environmental and economic assessment for the municipality of Aarhus (Denmark). *Waste Management, 30*(5), 744–754.

Lofthouse, V., Bhamre, T., & Trimingham, R. (2007). WR0113: Refillable packaging systems: Key methods and processes, WRT151: Objective 6.2, 1–31, DEFRA.

Pietrs, R. G. (1991). Changing garbage disposal patterns of consumers: Motivation, ability, and performance. *Journal of Public Policy & Marketing, 10*(2), 59–76.

Reschovsky, J. D., & Stone, S. E. (1994). Market incentives to encourage household waste recycling: Paying for what you throw away. *Journal of Policy Analysis and Management, 13*(1), 120–139.

Saphores, J. D. M., Nixon, H., Ogunseitan, O. A., & Shapiro, A. A. (2006). Household willingness to recycle electronic waste an application to California. *Environment and Behavior, 38*(2), 183–208.

Sidique, S. F., Lupi, F., & Joshi, S. V. (2010). The effects of behavior and attitudes on drop-off recycling activities. *Resources, Conservation and Recycling, 54*(3), 163–170.

Todd, P. M., & Gigerenzer, G. (2012). *Ecological rationality: Intelligence in the world*. Oxford: Oxford University Press.

Tucker, D., & Spiers, D. (2003). Attitudes and behavioural change in household waste management behaviour. *Journal of Environmental Planning and Management, 46*(12), 289–307.

Underwood, R. L., & Klein, N. M. (2002). Packaging as brand communication: Effects of product pictures on consumer responses to the package and brand. *Journal of Marketing Theory and Practice, 10*(4), 58–68.

Vining, J., & Ebreo, A. (1990). What makes a recycler? A comparison of recyclers and nonrecyclers. *Environment and Behavior, 22*(1), 55–73.

WRAP. (2007). *Understanding food waste—Research summary*. Available at http://www.wrap.org.uk/sites/files/wrap/Household_food_and_drink_waste_in_the_UK_-_report.pdf, March 2018.

CHAPTER 4

Prevention and Recycling Behaviours Across the EU

Abstract This chapter investigates the correlation between individual motivation and households' waste minimization and recycling. Individuals act based upon intrinsic and extrinsic motivation, the first one being something that comes from within the person itself and the second being conditioned on the receiving of an external reward. We aim to assess if one type of motivation is more correlated with one of the two behaviours (minimization and recycling) or the other. Using Eurobarometer data, we note that extrinsic motivation has a higher effect on sorting habits than on minimization behaviour while the reverse is true for intrinsic motivation. Conversely, intrinsic motivation plays a major role in prevention and for the recycling of particular kind of wastes such as hazardous waste.

Keywords Minimization behaviour · Hazardous waste recycling Eurobarometer

4.1 Introduction and Research Settings

The present chapter aims to shed some light on the correlation between individual motivation and households' waste minimization and recycling performances. The literature review presented in Chapter 2 outlined that, in general, individuals act based upon intrinsic and extrinsic motivation, the first one being something that comes from within the

© The Author(s) 2018   39
M. Gilli et al., *Household Waste Management*,
https://doi.org/10.1007/978-3-319-97810-9_4

person and the second one being conditioned on receiving of an external reward. Whilst it is certainly true that an individual is moved by a mix of both these motivations, the aim of this chapter is to verify if one type of motivation is more correlated with one of the two behaviours (minimization and recycling) or the other.

This question arises by considering what emphasized in Chapter 2, namely the different nature of the two actions. Whilst minimization cannot be directly observed from outside the person, i.e. is a hidden action, recycling has a measurable outcome. Everyone, for instance, can directly see if a household covered by a curbside collection scheme is recycling or not by watching what is in front of his doorstep. Therefore, we believe that recycling will be more sensitive to changes in external incentives, like for instance social norms and peer approval, with respect to minimization behaviour. Following on this reasoning, we expect minimization, on the contrary, to be less correlated to external incentives, being a type of pro-social behaviour, which generally happens inside the wall of a household living space (and consequently a hidden action). Similarly, unit pricing systems, and all the tariff schemes in which consumers pay for the collection of unsorted waste only, are expected to have a stronger effect on recycling with respect to minimization. Under such schemes, if a consumer recycles, the incentive to have a reduced fee is clear and direct, as more recycling means less unsorted waste. The capacity of these tariff schemes to support and incentivize minimization, on the contrary, is less clear, as the benefit of less waste production is harder to quantify (in term of reduction in the fee) to consumer. Summarizing, we can say that the two waste behaviours, recycling and minimization, are expected to respond differently to external pressure, an hypothesis which can be summarized in the following proposition:

H1: *Extrinsic motivations have a stronger effect on recycling than on waste minimization.*

The impact of intrinsic motivations follows a similar type of reasoning. If we start from the simple assumption that both recycling and minimization are costly and time-consuming activities for households, it is natural to deduce that more intrinsically motivated people are more likely to minimize waste and to recycle. We do expect, however, this effect to change both between minimization and recycling, and across the recycling of different materials. In particular, we believe that a certain level of intrinsic motivations is a precondition of waste minimization. If research hypothesis one is true, i.e. extrinsic motivations have a stronger effect on recycling behaviour, it comes as a consequence that in order to have minimization, individuals need to be moved by 'something' which comes from within themselves: the intrinsic motivations. Similarly, motivations can play a different role with respect to the recycling of different type of materials. Whilst paper, glass and plastic have been among the first products to be separately collected and may now be somehow part of the daily household waste management practices, some particular products such as medicines or e-waste might still require some effort to be correctly sorted. For example, recycling hazardous waste such as paint or batteries is generally associated with higher cost for individuals, as it requires them to drive to the closest civic amenity site. Formally we aim to test the following hypothesis:

H2: *The effect of intrinsic motivations is stronger in more costly recycling activities, like batteries, and in waste minimization activities.*

The chapter is organized as follows: Sect. 2 will describe the data and the methodologies applied; Sect. 3 will present and discuss the results, whilst Sect. 4 will conclude.

4.2   EMPIRICAL FRAMEWORK

4.2.1   *Data and Descriptive Evidence*

In order to conduct our empirical analysis, we exploited the Flash Eurobarometer 388 'Attitudes of Europeans towards Waste Management and Resource Efficiency' (FL 388), which is a survey carried out by the European Commission in 28 EU Member States at the end of 2013.[1] Flash Eurobarometers are a series of thematic surveys conducted to investigate attitudes and reactions of social groups to specific matters. This particular survey seems to be especially suitable

---

[1] Even though the data used in this chapter are collected and made available by the European Commission, we specify that, following the EU Decision on the use of Commission documents (12 December 2011), the results and their interpretation do not reflect the position of the Commission. Every comment included in this chapter is attributable only to the authors of this book.

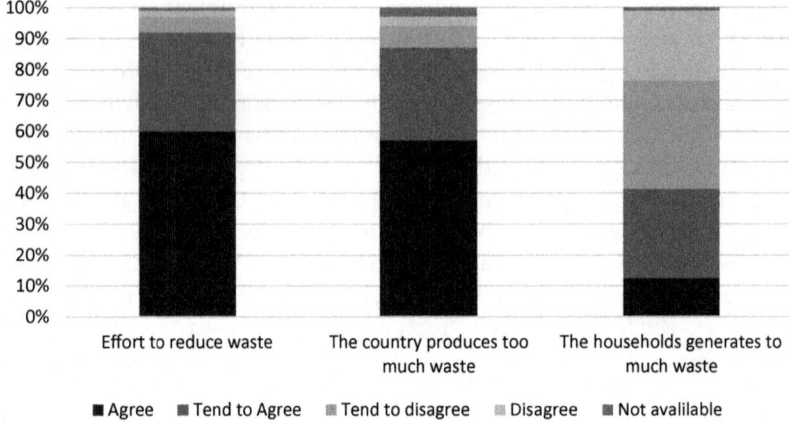

Fig. 4.1 Attitudes of EU citizens towards waste reduction (*Source* Flash Eurobarometer 388 Report [2014])

for our analysis for several reasons. Firstly, it covers exactly the topic we are discussing in this book, including both questions on motivations and on behaviours, that is, recycling and waste minimization. Secondly, the survey has been carried out in 28 EU Member states, and includes geographical and socio-economic characteristics of respondents, making it very suitable for an empirical analysis. Finally, such a broad coverage allows us to control for all these country- specific characteristics and preferences which may influence such a sensible topic as waste management.

Moving to the data, the FL 388 Report (European Commission 2014) underlines among the main findings that half of the European population believes that recycling and reducing waste is the best way to improve the use of resources throughout the EU. This is an interesting result in light of the transition towards a circular economy society (http://ec. europa.eu/environment/circular-economy/index_en.htm), which shows as European citizens are almost aware of the importance of this process. However, as Fig. 4.1 depicts, on the one hand, the majority of the EU citizens believe that their country is producing too much waste (57% in the second column), while on the other they believe their household is not significantly contributing (66% in the third column). Finally, the most of the surveyed population is making efforts to reduce waste (column 1).

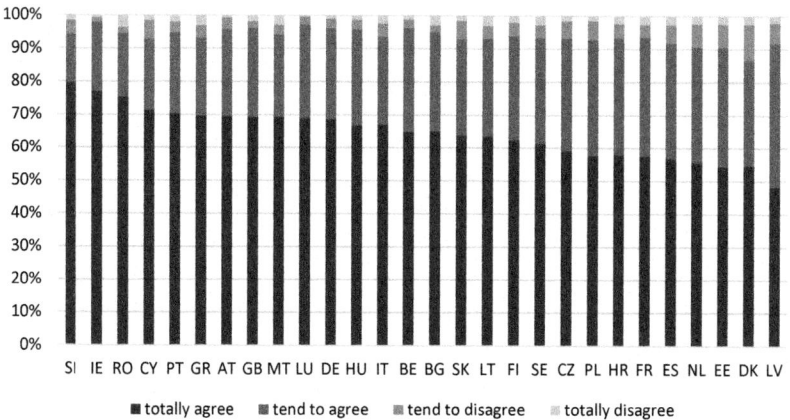

Fig. 4.2 Efforts to reduce waste as perceived by the respondents, by country (*Source* Own elaboration on FL 388 data)

Figure 4.2 depicts the perceived effort of waste reduction by country (more precisely, the question was asking to agree or disagree with a statement on efforts made by the household to reduce waste). The lower part of the bar indicates the proportion of the surveyed population who is inclined to make efforts to minimize their waste. A first thing to notice is that in line with the plot in Fig. 4.1 the majority of the population perceives to make effort for waste reduction and that the percentage is the highest in Slovenia, Ireland and Romania (80, 77 and 80%, respectively). However, even in the countries where this proportion is lower, the percentages are always around 50%. This may reflect that the EU population is aware of the problems generated by waste and on average willing to take care of their waste management. The highest share of people not inclined to reduce waste is found in Denmark and the Netherlands (12 and 10%, respectively) whilst the in the rest of the countries this proportion is always under 10%.

A clear pattern does not emerge for what concern waste minimization, which appears to be a more widespread practice across the EU member states with southern and eastern countries that show a higher proportion of respondents inclined to minimize their waste.

Figures 4.3, 4.4, and 4.5, represent the proportion of the sample that declared to recycle certain kinds of waste. Flash Eurobarometer 388

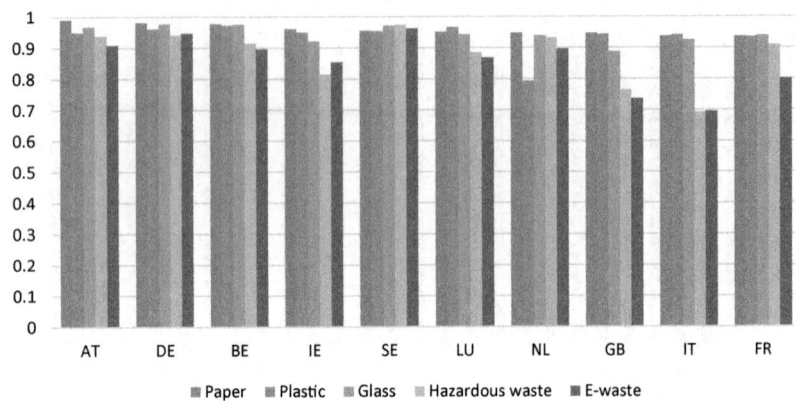

Fig. 4.3 Waste recycling by country (*Source* Own elaboration on FL 388 data. Countries (from the left): Austria, Germany, Belgium, Ireland, Sweden, Luxembourg, Netherlands, United Kingdom, Italy, France)

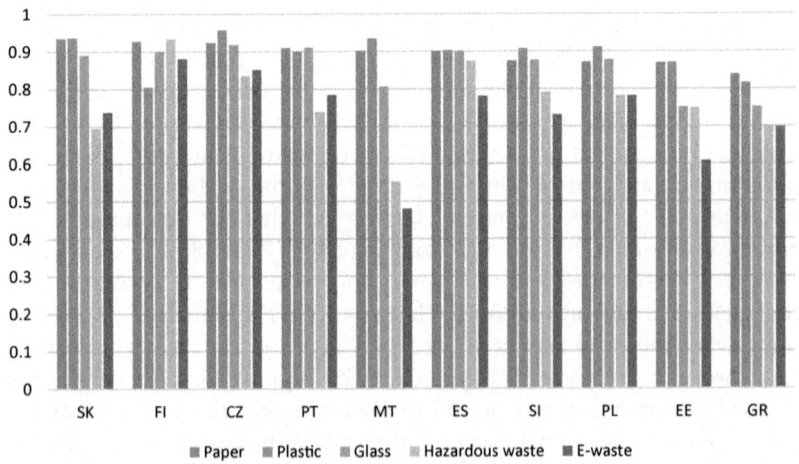

Fig. 4.4 Waste recycling by country (*Source* Own elaboration on FL 388 data. Countries (from the left): Slovakia, Finland, Czech Republic, Portugal, Malta, Spain, Slovenia, Poland, Estonia, Greece)

reports information on recycling of many waste materials (see Table 4.1 for a complete list). The kinds of waste chosen for the graph below can offer different insights on private separate collection. In fact, whilst

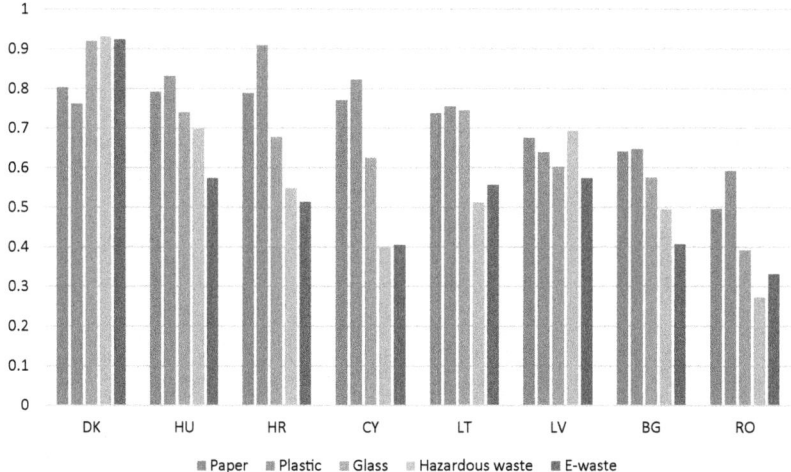

Fig. 4.5 Waste recycling by country (*Source* Own elaboration on FL 388 data. Countries (from the left): Denmark, Hungary, Croatia, Cyprus, Lithuania, Latvia, Bulgaria, Romania)

paper, plastic and glass have been recycled for a long time and might have become a usual practice in the management of the household, other kinds of waste such as hazardous wastes (e.g., oil used in the kitchen, paint) and e-waste (e.g., old electric appliances) still require some effort to be recycled, like for example going to the civic amenities. However, as shown in the figures and also noted by the Flash Eurobarometer 388 Report (2014), the sorting of paper, plastic and glass is very common in some countries (for example in Figs. 4.3 and 4.4 all countries except Greece report a percentage of 90% for sorting these wastes) and not common in others (as clearly shown in Fig. 4.5), where these proportion are below 70 or 60%. Hazardous wastes are sorted by the 90% of the surveyed population in Austria, Germany, Belgium, Sweden, France, Finland and Denmark. However, the majority of the respondents in other countries also declared to sort this kind of waste, with the exception of Romania where only less than the 30% of the sample sorts hazardous wastes. Northern EU countries also lead the way in sorting electronic waste, as shown by the figures. The lowest proportion of population that declares to sort e-waste is found in Romania, Cyprus, Bulgaria and Malta, with percentages around 30–40%.

Table 4.1 Descriptive statistics

Variables	Description	Obs.	Mean	Std. Dev.	Min.	Max.
Minimization variables						
Minwaste	Is a dummy variable that takes value 1 if the respondents declares to make efforts to minimize waste	26,595	0.930	0.255	0	1
Propensity to minimize	You make efforts to reduce the amount of waste that you generate:	26,595	1.466	0.733	1	5
	Totally disagree	526				
	Tend to disagree	1147				
	Tend to agree	7778				
	Totally agree	16,959				
	Not available	185				
Recycling variables						
Recwaste	Is a dummy variable that takes value 1 if the respondents declares to recycle at least 4 types of waste	26,595	0.964	0.186	0	1
Paper	Is a dummy variable that takes value 1 if the respondents declares to sort paper and cardboard	26,595	0.865	0.342	0	1
Plastic	Is a dummy variable that takes value 1 if the respondents declares to sort plastic materials	26,595	0.864	0.343	0	1
Glass	Is a dummy variable that takes value 1 if the respondents declares to sort glass	26,595	0.834	0.372	0	1
Hazardous	Is a dummy variable that takes value 1 if the respondents declares to sort hazardous waste	26,595	0.756	0.429	0	1
E-waste	Is a dummy variable that takes value 1 if the respondents declares to sort electrical waste (e-waste)	26,595	0.728	0.445	0	1

(continued)

Table 4.1 (continued)

Variables	Description	Obs.	Mean	Std. Dev.	Min.	Max.
Motivation variables						
Intrinsic motivations	Is a dummy variable that takes value 1 if the respondents declares that it is important to use resources more efficiently	25,425	0.956	0.205	0	1
	Yes	25,425				
	No	1170				
Extrinsic motivations	Is a dummy variable that takes value 1 if the respondent declares to prefer to pay waste management cost in proportion to the unsorted waste generated	23,976	0.956	0.205	0	1
	Yes	11,207				
	No	12,769				
Control variables						
Age	Age by categories:	26,595	3.152	0.966	1	4
	15–24	1967				
	25–39	4784				
	40–54	7078				
	55+	12,766				
Years of end of education	Years of education by categories:	26,595	2.529	0.908	1	6
	Up to 15	2781				
	16–19	9843				
	20+	12,155				
	Still studying	1344				
	No education	143				
	Refusal/not available	329				

(continued)

Table 4.1 (continued)

Variables	Description	Obs.	Mean	Std. Dev.	Min.	Max.
Occupation	Type of occupation	26,595	2.529	0.908	1	5
	Self-employed	2461				
	Employed	8243				
	Manual workers	1833				
	Not working	13,971				
	Refusal	87				
Household size	Household size by category:	26,595	2.284	1.002	1	6
	1	5851				
	2	11,837				
	3	4599				
	4+	4201				

To sum up, concerning the sorting of waste, there is a clear division among the EU member states, with northern EU that usually sort more waste and in higher percentage with respect to southern and eastern EU countries. In this latter group, waste separate collection appears to be a practice that still did not enter the households' management routines.

4.2.2   Methodologies

In order to empirically test hypotheses one and two reported above and based on the literature review in Chapter 2, we developed a simple empirical model. This can be achieved by adapting some of the questions of the FL 388 to a regression framework aimed to show the correlation between intrinsic and extrinsic motivations and waste minimization and recycling behaviours.

Table 4.1 describes and reports summary statistics for the selected variables.

Variables in Italic are our dependent variables; we selected two questions, related to minimization and sorting behaviour, respectively. For what concern minimization, the table shows that we considered two different variables. *Propensity to minimize*, as depicted in Fig. 4.2, is an ordered categorical variable which takes values from 1 to 4^2 as the propensity to minimize increases, i.e. as the answers passes from totally disagree (1) to totally agree (4). The other minimization variable, *minwaste* is a simple dummy variable that takes value 1 if the respondents had declared to make efforts to minimize and 0 otherwise.

For what concerns waste recycling behaviour, *recwaste* is our dependent variable. It is a dependent variable which takes value 1 if the respondents declare to sort at least 4 types of waste. Besides, we also considered the recycling of specific type of wastes, namely paper, plastic, glass, hazardous waste and e-wastes (electric and electronic wastes), and tested the effects of motivations on these categories alone. As explained in the data description section, we selected these particular kinds of waste because whilst paper, plastic and glass are generally recycled in relatively high share in Europe, we expect that the collection of hazardous and electrical waste still requires some efforts by households and so these might be a better indicator of the motivations behind behaviours.

---

[2] Values which are not available are considered as missing data in our data set.

The main regressors considered in this analysis are intrinsic motivations and extrinsic motivations. The first one is a dummy variable that takes value 1 if for the respondent it is important to use resources more efficiently. It is important to note, in this case, that the question was designed to detect the individual's level of awareness of the potential environmental threat deriving from an excessive use of resources and excessive waste generation.[3] On the basis of the analysis made in Chapter 2 (Sect. 2.3.1) we believe that a positive answer to this question underlies to some intrinsic motivations towards pro-environmental behaviour from the respondent.

Relatively to extrinsic motivations, we built the dummy variable by collecting the answer to a question related to the preferences of households related to the payment of the waste management costs. The variable takes value 1 if the respondent declares to prefer to pay the cost in proportion to the unsorted waste generated. Paying proportionally to the generated waste, in fact, can be an incentive to reduce waste in the first place, and to a better sorting of waste in the second place, with respect to, for example, paying a fixed amount through taxes.

Finally, we also included other control variables, related to demographic characteristics of the sample. We included the age of the respondents (in categories), the end of a respondents' education (in terms of age), occupation and household size. We note that the majority of the respondents are aged 55 or more and have studied until their twenties. The modal household size is 2.

4.2.3   The Model

To assess the effect of motivations on minimization and recycling behaviours we estimate the following equation:

$$y = \alpha + \beta_1 intrinsic + \beta_2 extrinsic + \beta_3 z + \varepsilon \qquad (4.1)$$

Where y is one of the dependent variables among *minwaste, propensity to minimize, recwaste, paper, plastic, glass, hazardous waste* and *e-waste;*

---

[3]We refer here to Q1 of the FL 388: 'The efficient use of resources means getting the greatest benefit out of scarce resources, such as metals, materials, land or water, while also causing less environmental damage. How important is it to you that Europe uses its resources more efficiently?'

intrinsic and *extrinsic* are the motivations varibles; z is a matrix collecting the control variables (age, end of education, occupation and household size) and country's fixed effect.

Moreover, following Chapter 2 we take into account the possibility of crowding-in and crowding-out effect by building a second model that includes and interaction term between intrinsic and extrinsic motivations, as in Eq. (4.2):

$$y = \alpha + \beta_1 intrinsic + \beta_2 extrinsic + \beta_3(intrinsic * extrinsic) + \beta_4 z + \varepsilon \quad (4.2)$$

Since the dependent variables are categorical in nature, we applied discrete choice model regression framework. In particular, for binary variables such as *minwaste, recwaste,* and *paper, plastic, glass* and hazardous and electrical waste, we choose binary logistic model, since the dependent can take only two values, 0 or 1. Results therefore are not interpreted as the marginal effect of, for example, intrinsic motivations on y but as the change in probability that y passes from 0 to 1 due to a change in *intrinsic motivations.* For propensity to minimize, we applied the ordered logit model, since the categories of these variables are ordered from less inclined to minimize to more inclined to minimize. Therefore, the results in this case are interpreted as a change in the probability of, for example, passing from 'tend to disagree' to 'tend to agree' to minimize waste due, for example to an increase in intrinsic motivations (intrinsic motivations passes from 0 to 1).

4.3   Correlation Between Motivations and Prevention and Sorting Behaviours

Table 4.2 shows the results related to waste minimization (columns 1 and 2) and propensity to minimize (columns 3 and 4).

Column 1 reports the coefficient in odds ratio for the model explained by Eq. (4.1). Here, we find that both intrinsic and extrinsic motivation has a positive and significant effect on a positive outcome for minimization, that is they increase the probability that a person decides to minimize. Given that the interpretation of odds ratio might not be intuitive, after we computed the probabilities associated with a positive outcome. We found that an intrinsically motivated person is more likely to reduce waste by 10% with respect to a person without any particular intrinsic motivation, whilst an extrinsically motivated person is likely to reduce waste by 1% with respect to a person who is not extrinsically

Table 4.2 Regression results (four different dependent variables)

	(1)	(2)	(3)	(4)
	Minwaste	Minwaste	Propensity to minimize	Propensity to minimize
Intrinsic motivations	1.124***	1.114***	0.575***	0.590***
	(0.094)	(0.118)	(0.077)	(0.102)
Extrinsic motivations	0.241***	0.218	0.180***	0.215
	(0.054)	(0.180)	(0.0278)	(0.151)
Intrinsic*Extrinsic		0.0258		−0.0361
		(0.188)		(0.153)
				(0.152)
Country dummy	Yes	Yes	Yes	Yes
Age	Yes	Yes	Yes	Yes
Employed	Yes	Yes	Yes	Yes
Years of education	Yes	Yes	Yes	Yes
Household size	Yes	Yes	Yes	Yes
Observations	23,976	23,976	23,840	23,840

Binary logistic estimations (column 1 and 2), ordered logit model (column 3 and 4). Robust standard errors in parentheses. Ordered logit estimations
*, **, ***indicate significance at 10, 5 and 1% levels, respectively

motivated. Even though both motivations serve the purpose of reducing the amount of produced waste, we notice that intrinsic motivations increase the probability of minimization nine times more than extrinsic motivations, a result in line with research hypothesis two.

When we consider possible crowding-in or crowding-out effects of motivations (Eq. 4.2) by including an interaction term between motivations, the results related to intrinsic motivations hold whilst extrinsic motivations are no longer significant. However, as it can be noticed from the standard error in parentheses and from the fact that the interaction term is not significant, these estimates are less efficient than the one column one. Therefore, estimates in column 1 are our preferred specification.

Colum 3 and 4 present the estimates relative to an increase in the propensity of minimization. In column 3, which shows our preferred specification, both intrinsic and extrinsic motivations have a positive and significant effect in increasing the propensity to reduce household waste. In terms of probability we found that an increase in intrinsic motivations increases the probability of passing from totally disagreeing to totally agreeing to reduce household waste by 13%, whilst extrinsic motivations increase these chances only by 4%.

Table 4.3 shows the results of the models in Eqs. (4.1) and (4.2) for recycling behaviour. As for the case of minimization behaviour and propensity to minimize, we note that the estimates with the interaction terms (Eq. 4.2; columns 2, 4, 6, 8, 10, and 12) are less efficient with respect to the estimates obtained from the model in Eq. (4.1), which is therefore our preferred specification.

A first thing to notice is that both motivations appears to be significant for recycling, even though there is heterogeneity in the magnitude of these effects. In general (column 1), an increase in intrinsic and extrinsic motivations positively affects the probability of recycling, by 9.2 and 2.2%. With respect to minimization, therefore, there is a lower effect of intrinsic motivations in increasing the probability of sorting behaviour and a higher effect of extrinsic motivations. This result is in line with our H1, which postulated that the effect of extrinsic motivations is higher for recycling behaviour than for minimization. For what concerns the other specific types of sorting, the effect of both kinds of motivations is significant and positive. In particular, for the most commonly recycled type of waste, on average the increase in recycling due to an increase in intrinsic motivations is around 10% (10% for paper, 7% for plastic and 9% for glass) whilst, as expected, the size of the effect becomes bigger for other materials. An increase in intrinsic motivations leads to a 12% increase in the probability of sorting hazardous waste and 11% increase in the probability of recycling e-waste. Relatively to extrinsic motivations, for paper, plastic and glass the effect of an increase in motivations is around 2% (1.9, 1.7 and 1.8%, respectively). On the contrary, the probability of recycling hazardous waste increases only by 1.4% whilst the effect probability of collecting e-waste is higher (2.3%).

To sum up, our analysis although simple, offers some interesting insights. First, we note that the effect of intrinsic motivations on the probability of minimization is higher than on the probability of recycling, except when considering particular types of waste such as hazardous waste and e-waste. In fact, on average, the probability of minimization increases by 10–11% whilst the probability of recycling increases by 8–9%. However, when considering the less frequently recycled wastes, such as dangerous waste and electrical waste, the probability of sorting given an increase in intrinsic motivations increases even by 12%. We believe that this result is driven by the fact that recycling these

Table 4.3 Regression results (four different dependent variables)

	(1)	(2)	(3)	(4)	(5)	(6)	(7)	(8)	(9)	(10)	(11)	(6)
	Recwaste	Recwaste	Paper	Paper	Plastic	Plastic	Glass	Glass	Hazardous waste	Hazardous waste	e-waste	e-waste
Intrinsic motivations	0.810***	0.851***	0.805***	0.821***	0.643***	0.654***	0.668***	0.722***	0.742***	0.740***	0.640***	0.699***
	(0.089)	(0.112)	(0.0843)	(0.106)	(0.0851)	(0.108)	(0.0840)	(0.106)	(0.0789)	(0.0993)	(0.0761)	(0.0960)
Extrinsic motivations	0.232***	0.338**	0.197***	0.238	0.170***	0.198	0.165***	0.300*	0.0994***	0.0952	0.151***	0.294*
	(0.043)	(0.177)	(0.0425)	(0.168)	(0.0419)	(0.168)	(0.0397)	(0.167)	(0.0346)	(0.157)	(0.0331)	(0.152)
Intrinsic* Extrinsic		−0.179		−0.0437		−0.0291		−0.144		0.00449		−0.151
		(0.157)		(0.173)		(0.173)		(0.172)		(0.160)		(0.156)
Country FE	Yes	Yes	Yes	Yes	Yes	Yes	Yes	Yes	Yes	Yes	Yes	Yes
Age	Yes	Yes	Yes	Yes	Yes	Yes	Yes	Yes	Yes	Yes	Yes	Yes
Employed	Yes	Yes	Yes	Yes	Yes	Yes	Yes	Yes	Yes	Yes	Yes	Yes
Years of education	Yes	Yes	Yes	Yes	Yes	Yes	Yes	Yes	Yes	Yes	Yes	Yes
Household size	Yes	Yes	Yes	Yes	Yes	Yes	Yes	Yes	Yes	Yes	Yes	Yes
Observations	23,203	23,203	23,976	23,976	23,976	23,976	23,976	23,976	23,976	23,976	23,976	23,976

Binary logistic estimations. Robust standard errors in parentheses. Ordered logit estimations

*, **, ***indicate significance at 10, 5 and 1% levels, respectively

particular kinds of waste requires more effort with respect to other types of waste, therefore this practice is more influenced by intrinsic motivations than extrinsic ones. The analysis of Chapter 5, will be specifically focused on this mechanism.

Extrinsic motivations, on the contrary, have a higher effect on recycling habits than on minimization behaviour. In fact, whilst the probability of minimization is increased by barely 1% if extrinsic motivations increase, when turning to recycling, this increase is around 2–3%. This is in line with what we postulated in the Chapter 2, that extrinsic motivations can be more effective in spurring recycling practices.

4.4   Conclusions

The aim of this chapter was to outline the relationship between individual motivations related to the environment and minimization and recycling behaviours.

Even though we are aware that a mix of the two motivations is what usually moves an individual, we aimed to investigate if one type of motivations is more related to minimization or recycling. In particular, given that minimization usually requires more effort and does not provide a measurable outcome, we related more closely intrinsic motivations to this kind of behaviour whilst hypothesized that extrinsic motivations can exert a stronger effect on recycling behaviour.

Moreover, given the great availability of information on the collection of different waste products, we also investigated if the recycling of materials that requires more effort (for example involving that the individual drops them to the civic amenity) are more influenced by intrinsic than by extrinsic motivations.

Results offer support to both our hypothesis. In fact, whilst we found that an increase in both intrinsic and extrinsic motivations has a positive and significant effect on the probability of both minimization and recycling, we noted that intrinsic motivations increase the probability to minimize than the probability of recycling. On average, the probability of minimization increases by 10–11% whilst the probability of sorting increases of 8–9% thanks to an increase in intrinsic motives. The reverse is true for extrinsic motivations, offering support to our first hypothesis (H1): whilst the probability of minimization is increased by barely 1% if extrinsic motivations increase, when turning to recycling, this increase is around 2–3%. Finally, concerning particular types of waste such as hazardous ones and e-wastes, our results show that in this case intrinsic motivations increase the chance to sort even by 12%, supporting our second hypothesis (H2).

To conclude, it is clear that a relation exists between pro-environmental attitudes and motivations. This chapter aimed to offer some insights on which behaviour is more influenced by a specific type of motivations. The next chapter will deepen the analysis by considering how motivations and policy related to waste management interact when looking at household separate collection performances.

Reference

European Commission. (2014). *Attitudes of Europeans towards waste management and resource efficiency.* Report on Flash Eurobarometer 388.

CHAPTER 5

Do Motivations Crowd in Recycling Policies? Evidence from Italy

Abstract This chapter, finally, considers both motivations and waste policies as determinants of people's waste-related behaviour, with a specific focus on recycling. It analyses how waste collection policies can incentivize household recycling behaviours and whether individual motivations are capable of crowding-in policy efficacies, especially when the efforts required by agents are high. We exploit a new survey of 618 Italian families that reports information on the opinions and stated actual recycling behaviours of the respondents with respect to five different waste materials. The results of our empirical analysis show that collection policies oriented at reducing time opportunity costs increase household recycling behaviours, and it is extremely relevant that policies are efficiently managed, lest discouraging effects occur. Moreover, individual motivations matter and may overcome possible weaknesses in waste policies, for example, by reducing the negative effects of 'distance' between households and recycling centres.

Keywords Recycling centres · Waste materials · Collection policies
Household recycling behaviours

M. Gilli et al., *Household Waste Management*,
https://doi.org/10.1007/978-3-319-97810-9_5

5.1   Introduction and Research Settings

The aim of the present chapter is to investigate whether motivations can be a necessary condition for the effectiveness of waste policies when household recycling is at stake. More specifically we are interested in verifying if individual motivations can overcome some of the possible weaknesses of the policies. As already emphasized in the previous chapters, recycling can be costly for households in terms of time opportunity costs, and given the high level of effort that complicated collection systems require, individual motivations can play a relevant role in fostering overall collection system effectiveness and consequently a country level of recycling.

The role of motivations as drivers behind individual decisions on waste management has been explored in Chapter 2, whilst Chapter 3 has been devoted to analysis of the effects that waste policies induce on individuals' waste-related behaviours. What we want here to more deeply investigate is the possible relationships among motivations and policies when household separate collection is considered. To that end we empirically test the interaction between motivations and policies and its effects on individual recycling behaviour by exploiting a new survey covering 618 Italian households. The survey reports the respondents' opinions and stated actual behaviours regarding recycling habits and waste production. The dataset appears to be particularly suitable for the purposes of our analysis.

As we previously highlighted in Chapter 3, different recycling programmes have pros and cons. It should be interesting to verify whether individual motivations play a role in overcoming the failings of recycling policies. What we are interested in is, for example, whether intrinsically motivated people are willing to recycle even if the distances from recycling centres are large or the collection frequencies are low.

More specifically, on the basis of the considerations made in the previous chapters, we formulate the following consequential research hypotheses that will be tested in the empirical analysis.

H1: *The higher the agent's effort required by a recycling programme, the higher individual motivations must be to induce separate collection.*

H2: *The lower the efficacy of each recycling programme, the higher the individual motivations must be to induce separate collection.*

5.2   EMPIRICAL FRAMEWORK

5.2.1   Data

Our empirical investigation is based on data from an original survey on waste behaviours of Italian households. From a methodological perspective, the survey was conducted through the integration of two different approaches: CAWI, computer assisted web interviews and CATI, computer assisted telephone interviews. The individuals analysed belonged to 618 Italian households, were representative of the whole population, and were stratified according to the following parameters: geographic macroarea, age and gender. The interviews were carried out between the 13 June 2014 and 19 June 2014. The respondent always was the head of the family or the adult responsible for domestic waste management.

The full list of variables exploited in the analysis and the original questions are presented in Table 5.11 in the Appendix. As dependents, we used five different ordinal variables that answer the following question: 'Do you collect waste separately?' Every question reflected a single different waste stream[1] and was assigned a value of 0 if the household was not collecting that type of waste separately, 1 if separately collecting that waste only 'sometimes', and 2 if collecting 'always'.

Among the regressors, the first set of variables reflected the degree of implementation of various waste policies. First, we included a proxy of information policies, labelled *specific knowledge*, which was assigned a value of 1 if the respondent believed that he or she had adequate information regarding the local separate collection scheme. Second, we assessed the role of collection policies by including three dichotomous choice variables that reflected the presence of *Curbside*, *Bring site* and *Civic-Amenities* in the municipality. It is worth noting that the variable *Bring site* is specific to each waste stream, whereas CA sites are, by definition, single areas for the collection of several waste streams. Figure 5.1 shows the diffusion of the three different collection instruments across our respondents. Interestingly, Bring site systems were well spread across the sample for all five materials; approximately 90% of households lived close to bring site systems specifically for paper and glass, whereas 75% had easy access to bring site systems for plastic, aluminium and organic wastes. In addition, curbside collection systems were well spread across

---

[1] Paper, Glass, Organic, Plastic, Aluminium.

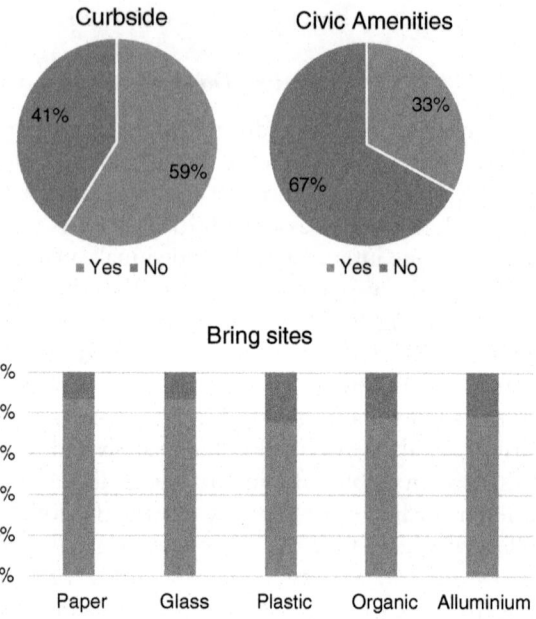

Fig. 5.1 Diffusion of the three collection policies across the analysed sample

Table 5.1 Share of households served by Bring Sites and Civic Amenities facilities that are also covered by a Curbside collection system

	Curbside	
	Yes (%)	*No (%)*
Bring site Paper	62	38
Bring site Glass	62	38
Bring site Organic	70	30
Bring site Plastic	70	30
Bring site Aluminium	68	32
Civic Amenities	60	40

the sample (59%), whereas Civic Amenities remained a residual disposal option (only 33%). Finally, the conditional occurrences of the different policy types are examined in Table 5.1. In particular, each line shows the share of households covered by different bring site systems or CA sites and that are also served by a curbside collection scheme. As the table

Table 5.2 Matrix of the correlations among the policy variables

	Curbside	Bring site Paper	Bring site Glass	Bring site Organic	Bring site Plastic	Bring site Aluminium	Civic Amenities
Curbside	1						
Bring site Paper	0.1756*	1					
Bring site Glass	0.1704*	0.8454*	1				
Bring site Organic	0.4042*	0.5807*	0.5578*	1			
Bring site Plastic	0.4198*	0.6157*	0.5825*	0.5659*	1		
Bring site Aluminium	0.3686*	0.7040*	0.7040*	0.6214*	0.6160*	1	
Civic Amenities	0.015	0.1239*	0.1128*	0.0638	0.1254*	0.0772	1

Note A * indicate significance at a 5% level

highlights, between 60 and 70% of the respondents covered by one type of bring site service also lived in an area served by a curbside system. The corresponding correlations among the policies were fairly high, as reported in Table 5.2. It is worth noting, however, that we always retained both *Curbside* and *Bring site* in our empirical analysis, despite their relatively high correlation, because we wanted to determine the net effect of each single policy once we controlled for the presence of all possible policy types.

Moreover, we included three different variables that reflected the levels of inefficacy of the three different policies (*Ineff Curbside, Ineff Bring Site* and *Ineff Civic Amenities*). The curbside variable reflects the frequency of collection, the variable for civic amenities reflects the distance between the households and collection point, and the variable for bring site systems indicates how often families find that recycling bins are full during a week and consequently cannot dispose their waste.

The other fundamental dimension investigated in our analysis is *Intrinsic Motivations*. On the basis of the analysis carried out in Chapter 2 (Sect. 2.3.1), we believe that at least three questions in our survey are suitable for this complex task. In the first question, which regards *food-waste*, we asked households how they feel when they waste food. This variable captures the individual disutility perceived from food-waste, which is expected to be higher for intrinsically motivated individuals (see D'Amato et al. 2016). For the second question, which regards *green-purchases*, we asked households whether they sustain firms that produce goods that use recyclable materials. This question represents personal environmental awareness and consciousness that we presume may influence the intensity of individual warm-glow. The choice of including variables related to general environmental awareness is in line with the literature that recognizes the significant role such awareness plays in shaping waste management decisions (see Chapter 2, Sect. 2.3.1). The third question follows the kind of proxy adopted in Cecere et al. (2014). It regards *waste-tax*, and a value of 1 is assigned if the individual does not prefer paying taxes to cover waste management based on the quantity generated (those who answered 'no') and 0 otherwise. It measures, in other words, whether individuals prefer to pay an amount based upon the quantity of waste that their household produces rather than paying for waste management through their taxes. The former response, which prices waste according to effective production, is more Pigouvian in style. The latter inclines more towards cost recovery strategies, funding public infrastructures (e.g. drop-off recycling centres) that support composting, recycling and proper disposal through waste taxes or tariffs.[2]

Despite the conceptual and theoretical foundations of these three questions, to test research hypotheses 1 and 2, we needed a single variable that reflects intrinsic motivations. We therefore aggregated the three items into a single index exploiting a generalization of principal component analysis (polychoric correlation matrix) due to Kolenikov and Angeles (2009). That method derives the correlation matrix used to build the principal components (PCs) by estimating the latent continuous variable that corresponds to each discrete or categorical variable, and, as a consequence, it is more suitable for our case, given the dichotomous or ordinal natures of our variables. The application of this technique to the three mentioned variables (*food-waste, green-purchase* and *waste-tax*) produced a single factor, labelled *intrinsic motivations*, that we used as an independent variable in our analysis.

Among the covariates, we controlled for the number of family members and house dimensions (squared metres), which may influence, on one hand, the compositions and amounts of total waste generated, and on the other hand, the opportunity costs of dedicating space for separate

---

[2]For a deeper explanation of the capability of this proxy to capture intrinsic motivations, see Chapter 2 (Sect. 2.3.1).

collection in apartments (expected to be lower in bigger houses). Moreover, we controlled for the respondents' social grades, which provide an indication of individuals' socio-economic positions based on occupation as a proxy for employment status.[3] It is in fact reasonable to suppose that time opportunity costs devoted to recycling efforts are affected by individual labour market characteristics. Finally, because education has been shown to positively influence recycling efforts (Duggal et al. 1991; Hong et al. 1993; Judge and Baker 1993; Reschovsky and Stone 1994; Callan and Thomas 1997; Jenkins et al. 2003), we included the educational levels of the respondents, which are expected to reflect and influence each respondent's overall environmental awareness.

5.2.2   *Empirical Protocol*

Empirically, given the nature of the dependent variable, we will refer to an ordered logistic regression. We note here that the 'distances' between the three outcomes (never, sometimes and always) are not equal. That primary difference must be borne in mind when interpreting the regression coefficients, which in this case do not represent a marginal effect. Technically, the coefficients were estimated through a maximum likelihood function, and the main regression table presents simple ordered log odds.

More specifically, we will be estimating the following baseline equation (Eq. 5.1):

Separate collection$_j$

$$= \alpha_i + \beta_1 \text{ mean intrinsic motivation} + \beta_2 \text{ specific knowledge} \quad (5.1)$$
$$+ \beta_3 \text{ curbside} + \beta_4 \text{ bring site}_j + \beta_5 \text{ CA Sites} + \beta_6 Z + \varepsilon,$$

where j refers to the above-mentioned five waste streams, i represents the 618 households and Z refers to the covariates summarized above. Given the chosen empirical framework, the regression coefficients need to be interpreted as follows: for a unit increase in mean intrinsic motivation (i.e. going from 0 to 1), we expect a β_1 increase in the ordered log odds of being in a higher group of separate collection behaviours (which

---

[3]This information is relevant in our case and in all cases plagued by the absence of reliable information on level of household income (see, for example, Hurst et al. 2014; Johns and Slemrod 2010; Pedace and Bates 2000).

are $0=$ 'never', $1=$ 'sometimes', and $2=$ 'always'), given that all of the other variables in the model are held constant. Moreover, this estimation technique also estimates two cut points (or thresholds), which correspond to the points on the latent variable that result in the different observed values on the dependent variable. It is worth noting that the interpretation of the ordered logit parameters does not depend on the cut points. Order logistic models are in fact based on the assumption that the relationships between pairs of outcome groups are the same, i.e. that the coefficient that describes the relationship between the first two categories (in our case, 'never' and 'sometimes') is the same as the one that describes the relationship between the second and third groups ('sometimes' and 'always'). If that condition does not hold, it cannot be correctly assumed, as the ordered logistic regression does, that a single model can suitably describe the latent response variable. To test that hypothesis, we employed an LR test, which tests the null hypothesis that there are no differences among the coefficients between models (Wolfe 1997). Alternatively, a Brant test of the parallel regression assumption, which verifies the same hypothesis, could be performed (Long and Freese 2003).[4] Tables 5.3, 5.4, 5.5, 5.6, 5.7, and 5.8 report the results for these two tests, which indicate that the proportional odds assumption has not been violated and that the ordered logistic model is suitable for our analysis.

Moreover, the main Eq. (5.1) will be augmented as follows in order to test for hypotheses 1 and 2:

Separate collection$_j$

$$
\begin{aligned}
= \alpha_i + \beta_1 \text{ mean intrinsic motivation} + \beta_2 \text{ specific knowledge} \\
+ \beta_3 \text{ curbside} + \beta_4 \text{ bring site}_j + \beta_5 \text{ CA Sites} \\
+ \beta_6 Z + \beta_7 \text{ mean intrinsic motivation} * \text{policy type} + \varepsilon,
\end{aligned}
\tag{5.2}
$$

and

Separate collection$_j$

$$
\begin{aligned}
= \alpha_i + \beta_1 \text{ mean intrinsic motivation} + \beta_2 \text{ specific knowledge} \\
+ \beta_3 \text{ curbside} + \beta_4 \text{ bring site}_j + \beta_5 \text{ CA Sites} + \beta_6 Z \\
+ \beta_8 \text{ mean intrinsic motivation} * \text{policy inefficiency} + Z\varepsilon.
\end{aligned}
\tag{5.3}
$$

[4]More information is available on the SPost9: http://www.indiana.edu/~jslsoc/web_spost9/sp_install.htm.

Table 5.3 Regression results (Paper)

	(1)	(2)	(3)	(4)	(5)	(6)	(7)	(8)	(9)
Curbside	1.043***	3.461***	0.445	0.161	1.000***	1.176***	0.453	0.868**	1.141***
Bring site (Paper)	1.173***	1.997***	1.003**	1.112***	-0.763	1.471***	1.162***	0.986**	1.376***
Civic Amenities	-0.114	0.0115	-0.568	-0.0994	-0.0280	-5.354***	-0.146	-0.0928	-0.329
Curbside * Bring Site		-3.026***							
Intrinsic Motivation	1.663***	1.975***	2.003***	1.305**	0.683	0.920	1.352**	2.769*	1.064*
Specific Knowledge	1.470***	1.427***	1.483***	1.492***	1.443***	1.544***	1.525***	1.462***	1.517***
Ineff Curbside			-0.214				0.0274		
Ineff Bring Site			-0.394***					-0.630*	
Ineff Civic Amenities			-0.131						1.401**
Intrinsic Motivation * Curbside				0.912					
Intrinsic Motivation * Bring Site					2.094**				
Intrinsic Motivation * Civic Amenities						5.151***			
Intrinsic Motivation * Ineff Curbside							-0.333		
Intrinsic Motivation * Ineff Bring Site								0.215	
Intrinsic Motivation * Ineff Civic Amenities									-1.455***
Constant cut1	-0.107	0.418	0.842	-0.461	-0.929	-0.429	-0.361	1.646	-0.434
Constant cut2	1.563	2.220**	2.620**	1.196	0.760	1.306	1.282	3.454**	1.287
LR test ($p > \chi^2$)	0.2087	0.2087	0.4588	0.3348	0.2352	0.1991	0.4588	0.2968	0.2734
Brant test ($p > \chi^2$)	0.159	0.159	0.533	0.115	0.175	0.268	0.533	0.290	0.394
Observations	371	371	354	371	371	371	370	355	371

Ordered logit estimations. *, **, ***indicate significance at 10%, 5% and 1% levels, respectively. All regressions include income the following control variables: family size, schooling, social grade and household size

Table 5.4 Regression results (Glass)

	(1)	(2)	(3)	(4)	(5)	(6)	(7)	(8)	(9)
Curbside	0.381	2.741***	-0.946	2.567**	0.360	0.446	-1.057	0.290	0.457
Bring site (Glass)	1.938***	2.943***	1.814***	2.048***	0.515	2.270***	2.162***	1.756***	2.222***
Civic Amenities	-0.148	-0.0244	-0.495	-0.195	-0.101	-5.632***	-0.243	-0.230	-0.0898
Curbside * Bring Site		-3.188***							
Intrinsic Motivation	1.096*	1.286**	1.779***	2.033***	0.573	0.242	2.191***	3.290**	0.333
Specific Knowledge	1.077***	0.949**	1.029**	1.025***	1.107***	1.137***	1.053**	0.989**	1.104***
Ineff Curbside			-0.616						
Ineff Bring Site			-0.470***				-1.830**	-0.972**	
Ineff Civic Amenities			-0.0475						1.792***
Intrinsic Motivation * Curbside				-2.205*					
Intrinsic Motivation * Bring Site					1.452				
Intrinsic Motivation * Civic Amenities						5.382***			
Intrinsic Motivation * Ineff Curbside							1.163**		
Intrinsic Motivation * Ineff Bring Site								0.479	
Intrinsic Motivation * Ineff Civic Amenities									-1.757***
Constant cut1	0.640	0.890	2.096*	1.453	0.260	0.264	1.687	3.549*	0.283
Constant cut2	2.254**	2.657**	3.909***	3.132***	1.872*	1.952*	3.370***	5.417***	1.958*
LR test ($p > \chi^2$)	0.2087	0.2087	0.4588	0.3348	0.2352	0.1991	0.4588	0.2968	0.2734
Brant test ($p > \chi^2$)	0.159	0.159	0.533	0.115	0.175	0.268	0.533	0.290	0.394
Observations	371	371	354	371	371	371	370	355	371

Ordered logit estimations. *, **, ***indicate significance at 10%, 5% and 1% levels, respectively. All regressions include income the following control variables: family size, schooling, social grade and household size

Table 5.5 Regression results (Organic)

	(1)	(2)	(3)	(4)	(5)	(6)	(7)	(8)	(9)
Curbside	1.422***	2.745***	0.0212	1.529	1.404***	1.431***	0.166	1.495***	1.432***
Bring site (Organic)	2.413***	2.921***	2.348***	2.419***	0.741	2.447***	2.472***	2.349***	2.426***
Civic Amenities	−0.141	−0.0988	−0.207	−0.142	−0.107	−1.231	−0.165	−0.154	−0.0267
Curbside * Bring Site		−1.809**							
Intrinsic Motivation	1.370***	1.617***	1.722***	1.422**	0.840	1.184**	1.490**	3.740***	1.276**
Specific Knowledge	0.855***	0.784***	0.827***	0.854***	0.834***	0.857***	0.872***	0.802***	0.858***
Ineff Curbside			−0.696**				−0.590		
Ineff Bring Site			−0.0976					−0.743*	
Ineff Civic Amenities			0.00832						0.230
Intrinsic Motivation * Curbside				−0.107					
Intrinsic Motivation * Bring Site					1.611				
Intrinsic Motivation * Civic Amenities						1.030			
Intrinsic Motivation * Ineff Curbside							0.0164		
Intrinsic Motivation * Ineff Bring Site								0.584	
Intrinsic Motivation * Ineff Civic Amenities									−0.183
Constant cut1	3.166***	3.323***	3.820***	3.221***	2.601***	3.006***	3.317***	6.032***	3.079***
Constant cut2	4.209***	4.419***	4.820***	4.265***	3.650***	4.051***	4.352***	7.051***	4.122***
LR test ($p>\chi^2$)	0.2087	0.2087	0.4588	0.3348	0.2352	0.1991	0.4588	0.2968	0.2734
Brant test ($p>\chi^2$)	0.159	0.159	0.533	0.115	0.175	0.268	0.533	0.290	0.394
Observations	371	371	354	371	371	371	370	355	371

Ordered logit estimations. *, **, ***indicate significance at 10%, 5% and 1% levels, respectively. All regressions include income the following control variables: family size, schooling, social grade and household size

Table 5.6 Regression results (Plastic)

	(1)	(2)	(3)	(4)	(5)	(6)	(7)	(8)	(9)
Curbside	0.234	1.669***	−0.372	−0.0990	0.202	0.259	−0.121	0.0500	0.226
Bring site (Plastic)	1.291***	1.949***	1.344***	1.260***	0.646	1.403***	1.253***	1.267***	1.440***
Civic Amenities	−0.335	−0.290	−1.453*	−0.328	−0.317	−3.108**	−0.347	−0.334	−1.339*
Curbside * Bring Site		−2.044***							
Intrinsic Motivation	1.691***	1.998***	1.879***	1.527***	1.420**	1.237**	1.341**	1.169	1.234**
Specific Knowledge	0.684**	0.623**	0.549*	0.688**	0.681**	0.708**	0.711**	0.599*	0.657**
Ineff Curbside			−0.177				0.107		
Ineff Bring Site			−0.397***					−0.214	
Ineff Civic Amenities			−0.358						0.672
Intrinsic Motivation * Curbside				0.343					
Intrinsic Motivation * Bring Site					0.651				
Intrinsic Motivation * Civic Amenities						2.667**			
Intrinsic Motivation * Ineff Curbside							−0.283		
Intrinsic Motivation * Ineff Bring Site								−0.215	
Intrinsic Motivation * Ineff Civic Amenities									−0.959**
Constant cut1	0.980	1.243	1.938*	0.811	0.701	0.709	0.637	1.305	0.682
Constant cut2	1.917**	2.206**	2.948***	1.747*	1.636*	1.656*	1.557	2.327	1.636*
LR test ($p>\chi^2$)	0.2087	0.2087	0.4588	0.3348	0.2352	0.1991	0.4588	0.2968	0.2734
Brant test ($p>\chi^2$)	0.159	0.159	0.533	0.115	0.175	0.268	0.533	0.290	0.394
Observations	371	371	354	371	371	371	370	355	371

Ordered logit estimations. *, **, ***indicate significance at 10%, 5% and 1% levels, respectively. All regressions include income the following control variables: family size, schooling, social grade and household size

Table 5.7 Regression results (Aluminium)

	(1)	(2)	(3)	(4)	(5)	(6)	(7)	(8)	(9)
Carbside	0.809***	2.178***	0.0769	0.817	0.782***	0.845***	−0.161	0.689**	0.879***
Bring site (Aluminium)	1.361***	1.833***	1.330***	1.362***	0.0823	1.518***	1.412***	1.303***	1.512***
Civic Amenities	0.233	0.287	1.042	0.233	0.283	−3.346**	0.216	0.218	1.185
Carbside * Bring Site		−1.791**							
Intrinsic Motivation	0.706	0.905*	1.013*	0.709	0.266	0.148	0.753	1.923	0.238
Specific Knowledge	1.088***	0.985***	1.154***	1.088***	1.072***	1.118***	1.106***	1.091***	1.134***
Ineff Carbside			−0.294				−0.468		
Ineff Bring Site			−0.427***					−0.718*	
Ineff Civic Amenities			0.275						1.343**
Intrinsic Motivation * Carbside				−0.00768					
Intrinsic Motivation * Bring Site					1.257				
Intrinsic Motivation * Civic Amenities						3.406***			
Intrinsic Motivation * Ineff Carbside							0.0303		
Intrinsic Motivation * Ineff Bring Site								0.268	
Intrinsic Motivation * Ineff Civic Amenities									−0.993**
Constant cut1	0.0614	0.243	1.351	0.0647	−0.356	−0.301	0.126	2.309	−0.256
Constant cut2	1.402	1.629*	2.826***	1.405	0.989	1.067	1.458	3.805**	1.104
LR test ($p > \chi^2$)	0.2087	0.2087	0.4588	0.3348	0.2352	0.1991	0.4588	0.2968	0.2734
Brant test ($p > \chi^2$)	0.159	0.159	0.533	0.115	0.175	0.268	0.533	0.290	0.394
Observations	371	371	354	371	371	371	370	355	371

Ordered logit estimations. *, **, ***indicate significance at 10%, 5% and 1% levels, respectively. All regressions include income the following control variables: family size, schooling, social grade and household size

Table 5.8 Regression results (Full Sample)

	(1)	(2)	(3)	(4)	(5)	(6)	(7)	(8)	(9)
Curbside	0.768***	2.512***	-0.00792	0.759*	0.799***	0.906***	-0.0179	0.726***	0.904***
Bring site (Waste Specific)	1.743***	2.303***	1.643***	1.677***	-0.250	1.803***	1.722***	1.633***	1.784***
Civic Amenities	-0.110	-0.0376	-0.325	-0.104	-0.0470	-3.447***	-0.124	-0.120	-0.103
Curbside * Bring Site		-2.231***							
Intrinsic Motivation	1.209***	1.510***	1.559***	1.199***	0.503*	0.703***	1.278***	2.576***	0.773***
Specific Knowledge	0.953***	0.954***	1.009***	1.035***	1.021***	1.048***	1.051***	1.001***	1.034***
Ineff Curbside			-0.355***				-0.393***		
Ineff Bring Site			-0.295***					-0.619***	
Ineff Civic Amenities			-0.0461						1.010***
Intrinsic Motivation * Curbside				0.0886					
Intrinsic Motivation * Bring Site					1.927***				
Intrinsic Motivation * Civic Amenities						3.215***			
Intrinsic Motivation * Ineff Curbside							-0.00797		
Intrinsic Motivation * Ineff Bring Site								0.293*	
Intrinsic Motivation * Ineff Civic Amenities									-0.972***
Constant cut1	1.218***	1.419***	2.203***	1.101***	0.460	0.759**	1.255***	3.275***	0.804**
Constant cut2	2.374***	2.595***	3.364***	2.218***	1.585***	1.894***	2.362***	4.457***	1.936***
LR test ($p>\chi^2$)	0.0396	0.0255	0.1304	0.0742	0.0090	0.0866	0.1389	0.0965	0.1127
Brant test ($p>\chi^2$)	0.043	0.052	0.177	0.084	0.012	0.104	0.190	0.098	0.129
Observations	1855	1975	1890	1975	1975	1975	1970	1895	1975

Ordered logit estimations. *, **, ***indicate significance at 10%, 5% and 1% levels, respectively. All regressions include income the following control variables: family size, schooling, social grade and household size. All regression incudes material fixed-effect

In particular, in Eq. (5.2), a significant and positive coefficient for β_7 means that research hypothesis 1 holds, i.e. intrinsic motivations are in a way capable of mitigating the individual efforts implied by the recycling policy. Similarly, β_8 in Eq. (5.3) is the parameter of interest for verifying hypothesis 2. For example, we remember here that the interaction term β_7 represents the effects of different policies (*Curbside*; *Bring Site*; *Civic-Amenities*) for different levels of mean intrinsic motivation. More specifically, a positive and significant coefficient for β_7 indicates that the effects of the policies are stronger for high levels of intrinsic motivation than for lower levels of motivation. This holds because, in this case, the partial derivative of Eq. (5.2) with respect to the different policy options is equal to

$$\frac{\delta \text{ Separate Collection}}{\delta \text{ Policy}} = \beta_k + \beta_7 \text{ mean intrinsic motivation; for } k = 3, 4, 5. \quad (5.4)$$

Finally, we test the same set of hypotheses with an additional specification in which we merged all the data together in a single panel dataset that varies across families and materials and presents an aggregate effect of the estimated coefficients. This last approach allows us to check for the robustness of our results once we control for unobserved material-specific factors that do not vary across individuals (it is, for instance, easier to store paper at home, with respect to organic waste). Empirically, for this last estimate, we augmented the three equations above with material specific fixed-effects.

5.3   Results

The results for the regression analysis conducted on the three main equations are summarized in Tables 5.3, 5.4, 5.5, 5.6, and 5.7 for each of the different waste streams and in Table 5.8 for the aggregate specification. First, we note here that the covariates, when significant, always show the expected outcomes.[5]

Starting from the results on the implementations of the different waste collection programmes, we observe that the *bring site* systems are always positively correlated with recycling behaviour for each of the five

---

[5]We decided to not include the full list of covariates to ease the interpretation of the results. They are, however, available upon request.

kinds of materials considered. Oppositely, *civic amenities* are never significant. The effect of *curbside* access on household recycling varies by material type.[6] It is significant and positive except for glass and plastic. Moreover, as shown in the second columns of the regression tables, the *bring site* systems and *curbside* are always substitutes[7] with respect to recycling behaviours, confirming the previous work of Beatty et al. (2007). It is hence possible that households prefer to get rid of bulky materials such as plastic and glass at the nearest *bring site* centre rather than storing them for *curbside* collection. Moving to the information policies, *specific knowledge* always has a positive impact on recycling behaviour for all kinds of materials. Increasing information about correct separate collection implies reductions in time and effort by households and enhances their recycling behaviours. The other main variable of interest, *Intrinsic Motivation*, shows the expected positive coefficient and an overall statistical significance (except for aluminium).

Moving to our research hypotheses, when we consider the role that intrinsic motivations have in easing the individual efforts required by the different recycling programmes, we find interesting results. As seen above, both *bring site* and *curbside* are per se able to induce household recycling independently of individual motivations. The only collection programme in our sample that does not influence individual recycling behaviour is *civic Amenities*. The interesting result is that it is the only collection policy for which the interactions with intrinsic motivation is almost always statistically significant and positive (see column 6 in Tables 5.3, 5.4, 5.5, 5.6, and 5.7). The only exception is 'organic waste', which is a reasonable and expected result, considering that bio-waste is by its nature hard to transport. This result confirms our first research hypothesis. Actually, *civic amenities* is the recycling programme that requires the highest household effort and has a positive and significant effect on recycling behaviour only for individuals characterized by high intrinsic motivation.

---

[6] That different materials types matter when waste recycling is at stake is a result that is highlighted in other studies. In Beatty et al. (2007) and Jenkins et al. (2003), for example, the impact of increasing curbside access on recycled quantities varied across different materials.

[7] In our sample, households were served by both bring site and curbside programs in 62% of cases for glass and in 70% for plastic (see Table 5.1).

Considering the results regarding the inefficacies of the different recycling programmes, the most evident outcome is for *bring site*, whose inefficacy is always (except for organic waste) statistically significant and negative. It is worth remembering that for that specific programme, inefficacy reflects 'how often households find recyclable bins full during the week and are not consequently capable of disposing their waste'. Such events can induce discouraging effects on agents, who see their efforts hindered by a negligent waste collection system, to the point that the positive effect of a nearby bring site system on recycling behaviour is partially neutralized by that inefficacy.

Moving to the interactions between the intrinsic motivations and inefficacies of the policies, the results are not statistically significant for *ineff bring site*. This means that for that specific recycling policy, high levels of inefficiencies can also disincentivize the most committed agents. Our second research hypothesis cannot be accepted in the case of bring sites. However, in the case of *civic amenities*, once again motivations matter, and more motivated individuals are the only ones who are induced to increase their recycling through the presence of collection sites located very far from their own houses. Empirically speaking, in fact, the interaction term and the coefficient for *civic amenities* are always statistically significant, with an overall U-shaped effect. This means that, once accounting for the joint effect that intrinsic motivation has on CA sites, their effects turn out to be positive.

5.3.1   *Quantification*

The interpretation of the raw coefficients in Tables 5.3, 5.4, 5.5, 5.6, 5.7, and 5.8 is not straightforward, and the results should be read such that for a unitary increase in intrinsic motivation, in the case of paper waste, we expect a 1.663 increase in the ordered log odds of being in a higher level of our dependent variable, holding all other control variables constant. There are several common approaches to better quantify these results. In Table 5.9, for example, we transformed the raw coefficients in the proportional odds ratio, which can be interpreted as the odds ratio of the traditional logit model. In that case, the results for paper waste mean that for a unit increase in intrinsic motivation, we can expect a 5.277 increase in the odds ratio of being in the 'always' group with respect to the 'sometimes' group. Similarly, the same effect holds for the odds of being in the 'sometimes' group with respect to the 'never' group.

Table 5.9 Quantification. Benchmark specification: column 1 of Tables 5.3, 5.4, 5.5, 5.6, 5.7, and 5.8. All materials

	Paper		Glass		Organic		Plastic		Aluminium	
	Unit effect	SD effect	Unit effect	SD effect	Unit effect	SD effect	Unit effect	SD effect	Unit effect	SD effect
Door-to-door	2.838	67.0	1.464	20.6	*4.146*	*101.1*	1.263	12.2	2.246	48.8
Bring Site	*3.232*	*50.8*	*6.943*	*97.2*	*11.164*	*189.1*	*3.635*	*75.8*	*3.901*	*77.3*
Civic Amenities	0.892	−5.3	0.862	−6.8	0.868	−6.5	0.715	−14.8	1.262	11.7
Intrinsic Motivation	*5.277*	*54.2*	*2.992*	*33.0*	3.936	42.9	*5.423*	*55.3*	2.025	20.2
Specific Knowledge	*4.350*	*86.6*	*2.935*	*57.9*	2.351	43.7	1.982	33.7	*2.969*	*58.7*

Unit effect is the factor change in odds for unit increase in the different independent variables and is calculated taking the exponential value of regression coefficients. SD effect, is the percent change in odds corresponding to a standard deviation increase in the independent variables
Coefficients in italic are statistically significant (5%)

Moreover, to ease comparisons among the different effects, in Table 5.9, we also present the percent changes in the odds for standard deviation increases in the different independent variables for all materials, taking as a benchmark specification 1 in Tables 5.3, 5.4, 5.5, 5.6, 5.7, and 5.8. The advantage of this last transformation is that exploiting standard deviation variations in the independent variables allows comparisons of the magnitudes of the effects across variables and across samples. This simple transformation shows, for example, that the effects of *Bring Sites* were stronger for organic waste and glass, whereas intrinsic motivations had stronger effects for plastic and paper. Similarly, the results in Table 5.10 show the applications of the same transformations to specification 3 of Tables 5.3, 5.4, 5.5, 5.6, 5.7, and 5.8. Interestingly, with this last quantification, we can compare the effect of *Ineff Bring Site* with respect to that of *Bring Site* in order to understand whether the inefficiencies, where present, are capable of fully offsetting the positive effect of that waste policy. Overall, the coefficient of the *Bring Site* was generally twice the size of its inefficiency, suggesting that positive effects also tend to prevail in the presence of ineffective collection systems. A significant exception was paper waste, where the two effects had similar magnitudes, suggesting, once again, the importance of efficient collection services.

Table 5.10 Quantification. Benchmark specification: column 3 of Tables 5.3, 5.4, 5.5, 5.6, and 5.7. All materials

	Paper		Glass		Organic		Plastic		Aluminium	
	Unit effect	SD effect	Unit effect	SD effect	Unit effect	SD effect	Unit effect	SD effect	Unit effect	SD effect
Door-to-door	1.561	24.6	0.388	−37.4	1.021	1.1	0.690	−16.8	1.080	3.9
Bring Site	2.726	42.3	6.135	89.3	10.463	183.4	3.836	80.5	3.779	75.8
Civic Amenities	0.566	−23.8	0.610	−21.1	0.813	−9.4	0.234	−50.1	2.834	64.6
Intrinsic Motivation	7.413	69.5	5.921	59.8	5.594	57.4	6.544	64.0	2.753	30.6
Specific Knowledge	4.408	86.6	2.798	54.2	2.285	41.6	1.732	26.0	3.172	62.5
Ineff Door-to-door	0.807	−23.3	0.540	−53.3	0.499	−57.7	0.838	−19.7	0.746	−30.5
Ineff Bring Site	0.674	−41.3	0.625	−47.0	0.907	−12.4	0.672	−41.5	0.653	−43.8
Ineff Civic Amenities	0.877	−19.2	0.954	−7.5	1.008	1.4	0.699	−44.2	1.316	56.5

Unit effect is the factor change in odds for unit increase in the different independent variables and is calculated taking the exponential value of regression coefficients. SD effect, is the percent change in odds corresponding to a standard deviation increase in the independent variables
Coefficients in italic are statistically significant (5%)

Finally, Fig. 5.2 presents a graphical representation of the significant interactions between civic amenities and intrinsic motivation, which are probably the most interesting results obtained with regard to research hypothesis 1. In all instances, with the exception of glass, it is evident that the effect of civic amenities depends heavily on the level of intrinsic motivations, being negative when intrinsic motivation is 'low' and positive when intrinsic motivation is 'high'. The gap between the two effects is wider for plastic and aluminium, which are typically collected in drop-off centres in Italy. In contrast, the two lines shown in the figure are closer for paper waste and nearly overlap in the case of glass waste. This result is in line with expectations and stresses that the overall efficacy of civic amenities depends on the material considered. Overall, the effect of civic amenities is weaker for paper and glass waste, two waste streams that are generally collected using door-to-door systems, suggesting, once again, that different disposal choices might be rivals with respect to separate collection performances.

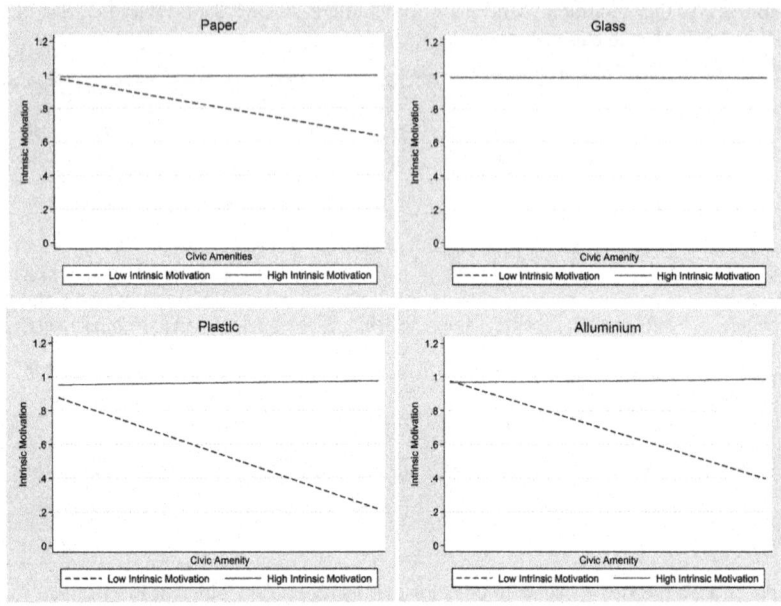

Fig. 5.2 Interaction between Intrinsic Motivation and Civic Amenities

5.4 CONCLUDING REMARKS

In this chapter, analyses have been presented on how single recycling policies can incentivize household recycling behaviours and whether individual motivations matter in crowding-in these policies, especially when the efforts required by agents are high.

The empirical analysis, which was conducted on a sample of 618 Italian households, provided interesting outcomes and arguments that are potentially relevant for policy. First, bring site and curbside recycling programmes were found to be capable of incentivizing the recycling behaviours of individuals. That outcome confirms for our sample what has already been highlighted in the literature; recycling behaviours are positively affected by policies that reduce opportunity costs in terms of time spent by individuals. Moreover, in our sample, the two programmes' are substitute, which invites policymakers to consider potential trade-offs between the two waste policies, as has been already emphasized

(Beatty et al. 2007). Another important result is that it is not sufficient to provide bring sites, but it is absolutely necessary that they be efficiently managed. In fact, the eventuality that recycling bins are full counterbalances the initial incentivizing effect, pushing individuals to reduce their recycling behaviours. The efforts households devote to recycling must be compensated by good maintenance of the bring sites. The result is even stronger because it remains true for highly motivated people as well.

Second, information policies in our sample matter. Good information on what and where to separately collect implies time savings for individuals and incentivizes their recycling behaviours. More care should be given to spreading specific knowledge, both through information campaigns conducted by single municipalities and through information notes reported by producers on product packaging.

Third, individual motivations play a relevant role in boosting recycling and can crowd in the recycling programme that in our study requires the highest effort by the agents, i.e. Civic Amenities. In fact, the presence of this kind of drop-off system only incentivizes the recycling behaviours of motivated households, even in cases of large distances from their houses. This result provides food for thought for policymakers when designing policy instruments such as CA Sites and suggests that this tool can be very effective in highly intrinsically motivated areas but, on the contrary, is not at all beneficial for persons with low motivations. The economic rationale behind this result is straightforward; given the effort correlated with going to CA sites, only motivated agents have the inner incentive to exploit those collection areas. Moreover, if we change perspective, this result also suggests that campaigns to increase citizen awareness towards waste issues and increase their intrinsic motivations can also have positive effects on the profitability of CA sites.

In pursuing the aims of achieving a recycling society and long-term sustainability targets, the contributions of citizens are fundamental. In this sense, policies that reduce the cost of recycling in terms of individual effort are relevant, and their effectiveness may even be improved with government educational and information campaigns aimed at increasing individuals' awareness of environmental and waste problems.

Appendix

See Table 5.11.

Table 5.11 Variables and main descriptive statistics

Variable name	Question in the survey	Mean	St. dev.	Min.	Max.	Obs.
Recycling (Paper)	Do you collect Paper waste separately? (0 'never'; 1 'Sometimes'; 2 'Always')	1.79	0.51	0	2	618
Recycling (Glass)	Do you collect Glass waste separately? (0 'never'; 1 'Sometimes'; 2 'Always')	1.81	0.48	0	2	618
Recycling (Organic)	Do you collect Organic waste separately? (0 'never'; 1 'Sometimes'; 2 'Always')	1.57	0.74	0	2	618
Recycling (Plastic)	Do you collect Plastic waste separately? (0 'never'; 1 'Sometimes'; 2 'Always')	1.67	0.66	0	2	618
Recycling (Aluminium)	Do you collect Aluminium waste separately? (0 'never'; 1 'Sometimes'; 2 'Always')	1.65	0.65	0	2	618
Specific Knowledge	Do you think your family received adequate information on the functioning of your local separate collection scheme? (1 'Yes'; 0 'No')	0.72	0.43	0	1	618
Curbside	Is your municipality covered by a curbside collection scheme? (1 'Yes'; 0 'No')	0.58	0.49	0	1	572
Bring Site (Paper)	Is there a Bring Site facility for Paper waste close to your house? (1 'Yes'; 0 'No')	0.86	0.33	0	1	618
Bring Site (Glass)	Is there a Bring Site facility for Glass waste close to your house? (1 'Yes'; 0 'No')	0.86	0.33	0	1	618
Bring Site (Organic)	Is there a Bring Site facility for Organic waste close to your house? (1 'Yes'; 0 'No')	0.77	0.41	0	1	618
Bring Site (Plastic)	Is there a Bring Site facility for Plastic waste close to your house? (1 'Yes'; 0 'No')	0.75	0.43	0	1	618
Bring Site (Aluminium)	Is there a Bring Site facility for Aluminium waste close to your house? (1 'Yes'; 0 'No')	0.78	0.41	0	1	618
Civic Amenities	Is there a civic amenity close to your house? (1 'Yes'; 0 'No')	0.32	0.46	0	1	552

(continued)

Table 5.11 (continued)

Variable name	Question in the survey	Mean	St. dev.	Min.	Max.	Obs.
Food-waste	How much do you dislike to throw away food? (from 5 'very dislike' to 0 'I do not care')	4.46	1.01	0	5	479
Green-purchase	Do you sustain firms which produce goods with recyclable materials (1 'Yes'; 0 'No')	0.72	0.44	0	1	618
Waste-tax	Do you prefer to pay a waste tax based on the quantity of waste generated? (0 'Yes'; 1 'No')	0.55	0.49	0	1	618
Ineff Curbside	How often are waste collected? (1 'once per week'; 2 'twice per week'; 3 'three times per week') Multiplied by −1 in the analysis	−1.33	1.24	−3	−1	571
Ineff Bring Site	How often how often do you find recyclable bins full during a week and are consequently not capable of disposing your wastes? (1 'Never'; 2 'infrequently'; 3 'once or twice per month'; 4 'once per week'; 5 'two or three times per week') Multiplied by −1 in the analysis	−3.01	1.34	−5	−1	585
Ineff Civic Amenities	How distant is the closest CA to your household (1 'more than 10 km'; 2 'between 5 and 10 km'; 3 'between 3 and 5 km'; 4 'minus of 3 km') Multiplied by −1 in the analysis	−1.03	1.58	−4	−1	551
Family Size	How many people are there in your family?	3.07	1.16	1	7	618
Schooling	Educational qualification? (Ranging from 1: 'Ph.D.' to 7 'Primary school')	4.26	1.78	1	7	618
Social Grade	Which is your main source of income? (1 'employee'; 2 'self-employ'; 3 'pension'; 4 'other allowances'; 5 'personal assets'; 6 'family'; 7 'other')	2.19	1.88	1	7	618
House Size	How big is your house/apartment? (1 'less than 50 m², 2 '50–74 m², 3 '75–99 m², 4 '100–124 m²; 5 '125–149 m², 6 '150–174 m², 7 '175–199 m², 8 'more than 200 m²')	3.78	1.72	1	8	574

REFERENCES

Beatty, T. K., Berck, P., & Shimshack, J. P. (2007). Curbside recycling in the presence of alternatives. *Economic Inquiry, 45*(4), 739–755.

Callan, S., & Thomas, J. (1997). The impact of state and local policies on the recycling effort. *Eastern Economic Journal, 23,* 411–423.

Cecere, G., Mancinelli, S., & Mazzanti, M. (2014). Waste prevention and social preferences: The role of intrinsic and extrinsic motivations. *Ecological Economics, 107,* 163–176.

D'Amato, A., Mancinelli, S., & Zoli, M. (2016). Complementarity vs substitutability in waste management behaviors. *Ecological Economics, 123,* 84–94.

Duggal, V. G., Saltzman, C., & Williams, M. L. (1991). Recycling: An economic analysis. *Eastern Economic Journal, 17*(3), 351–358.

Hong, S., Adams, R. M., & Love, H. A. (1993). An economic analysis of household recycling of solid wastes: The case of Portland, Oregon. *Journal of Environmental Economics and Management, 25*(2), 136–146.

Hurst, E., Li, G., & Pugsley, B. (2014). Are household surveys like tax forms? Evidence from income underreporting of the self-employed. *Review of Economics and Statistics, 96*(1), 19–33.

Jenkins, R. R., Martinez, S. A., Palmer, K., & Podolsky, M. J. (2003). The determinants of household recycling: A material-specific analysis of recycling program features and unit pricing. *Journal of Environmental Economics and Management, 45*(2), 294–318.

Johns, A., & Slemrod, J. (2010). The distribution of income tax noncompliance. *National Tax Journal, 63*(3), 397.

Judge, R., & Baker, A. (1993). Motivating recycling: A marginal cost analysis. *Contemporary Policy Issues, 11,* 58–68.

Kolenikov, S., & Angeles, G. (2009). Socioeconomic status measurement with discrete proxy variables: Is principal component analysis a reliable answer? *The Review of Income and Wealth, 55*(1), 128–165.

Long, J. S., & Freese, J. (2003). *Regression models for categorical dependent variables using Stata, revised edition.* College Station, TX: Stata Corporation.

Pedace, R., & Bates, N. (2000). Using administrative records to assess earnings reporting error in the survey of income and program participation. *Journal of Economic and Social Measurement, 26*(3, 4), 173–192.

Reschovsky, J. D., & Stone, S. E. (1994). Market incentives to encourage household waste recycling: Paying for what you throw away. *Journal of Policy Analysis and Management, 13*(1), 120–139.

Wolfe, R. (1997). *OMODEL: Stata modules to perform tests on ordered probit and ordered logit models* (Statistical Software Components S320901). Boston College Department of Economics.

INDEX

Printed by Printforce, the Netherlands